one night to get it right:
the making of an Independent film

Sebastian J. Howley

First Edition September 2010

The screenplay in this book is a work of fiction. Any names, characters, places or events are the product of the author's imagination or are used fictitiously. Any resemblance to actual persons, living or dead, events or locations is entirely coincidental.

Dedicated to my parents

USE OF THIS BOOK

This book is meant to provide insight into
the preparation and production of a low/no-
budget film. Although this book offers real
world advice from experience, it is not
meant to replace legal consul. Please
consult a lawyer or an accountant for all
business and financial decisions.

FOREWORD

It all started when an old friend of mine almost ran over my sister while he was running late for work. Tony and I have been friends for over twenty years but had lost touch in the last few. I had moved to Los Angeles, while Tony had moved around himself before settling back in Chicago. My sister had moved back just before I did to be closer to our father who was fighting terminal cancer. I moved back and found myself with lots of time on my hands and without knowing many people still in Chicago. I began writing to make good use of my time until I was able to make new connections. After months of late night writing sessions, I finally finished and published my first novel.

I felt a sense of accomplishment by finishing a novel but I had left Los Angeles without achieving my goal of getting a film produced. It was an easy choice to leave L.A. in order to be able to spend time with my father but I also had no purpose; I was lost. I had gotten a full-time job but it had no meaning to me. My father did not want me to waste whatever progress I had made when I moved out West. He let me know very clearly that under no circumstance should I put my life on hold. My parents instilled a strong work ethic in me and my father did not talk just for the sake of talking. A man of few words; he meant what he said.

I got out a notebook and made a list of all my resources. I collected and reviewed every script and idea I had. By reviewing my resources, I realized that almost everyone I knew had moved away from Chicago. Launching a film project would require starting from scratch for me, so I had a lot of work to do. Then one day in the fall of 2008, as I mentioned, Tony almost ran over my sister. He didn't know she had moved back to Chicago so he found her online and sent her an email. She mentioned that I had moved back as well, my first book was done and that I was not doing a lot at the moment. Tony got a hold of me and we went for coffee.

This coffee chat set in motion the next two years of my life. Tony had read my book and wanted to talk about my L.A. experiences. I got caught up on Tony's latest music projects, which brought us to what we were both doing at the moment: nothing. We were both doing nothing. I had recently hurt my back at my job and was seriously questioning what I was doing with myself. Whatever fears had stopped me from making a feature film before had to be defeated. I knew what I needed to do. So when he asked me what I was going to do now I was officially living in Chicago again, I said the magic words: "I want to make a movie." Without hesitation he said, "Let's do it." The question now of course was, "What movie should we make?"

I looked at the list of ideas I had kicking around my brain and decided on a romantic comedy. I felt that there were too many Independent films being made that were overly violent, based on zombie attacks or about some money-centered plot like a bank robbery or something. I felt the need to tell a story about people finding love in a troubled world. At the time, the economic spiral downward was beginning to affect the country by raising the level of anxiety in what seemed like everyone.

I originally wanted to make a more mainstream type of romantic comedy but it just didn't feel right to me. Making a more personal, less over-the-top comedy was going to limit the audience but I knew that it was the type of film I wanted to make. The original idea was also too large in scope as it took place over a few years. This was out of our range in terms of budget. The biggest change, at this point, was the decision to make the tone and style of the film more naturalistic and dramatic.

In order to simplify the scope of the film, the story would take place on a single night. By combining or eliminating smaller characters and locations, we were able to focus the story for a more manageable and limited budget. I finished the script fairly quickly as I connected with the characters and put a lot of myself into the story. Once the script was completed, we set up auditions at a theater and luckily we found the perfect cast. The actor's completely understood and embodied the characters right away. They fit so well in fact, the two actresses actually wore the same outfits they had on at the auditions in the movie.

Every film presents certain challenges and "One Night" was no exception. The first week of our filming my father went into the hospital with a rather bleak outlook. At this point, the complications from his terminal cancer were life threatening. I immediately began to figure out how to delay the filming at the last minute but my father wouldn't allow it. He refused to let me just sit in the room when there was work to be done. We went on as planned but every second I wasn't filming I was there with him and my family. He was released from the hospital and was set up at home with hospice care. I kept moving forward and we managed to complete filming the following month.

The editing process was an up-and-down rollercoaster ride, to say the least. In October of 2009, after completing the first rough cut of the film I decided to back-up the film. In the process of doing this the external hard drive containing all the files for the film crashed. It went down for the count. DEAD. The next morning I was going to show my dad the film but it was not to be. By the time I had the files recovered and re-edited the film, it was too late to show it to him. I had spent two months editing from scratch but sadly he died the day after I got it all put back together.

I did get to show him some scenes and he gave me a lot of good feedback.

I would be lying if I said I wasn't completely derailed by his death. I couldn't even think about the movie but giving up on it was obviously not an option. I decided to work as hard as I could to fix any and all problem areas with the film. I made a promise to myself that if it was humanly possible for me to make some aspect of the film better, I would do it. This was the start of the first big change for the film. I sat down and watched the film scene by scene and made a list of what I needed to change. We spent a few days filming some transition shots, re-filming one whole scene, I bought some stock footage and we re-recorded the audio for four complete scenes.

The second big change came after I began showing the film to family, friends and cast members. At that point, the film was black-and-white with only a minimal soundtrack. It looked fantastic but people felt the color clips I showed them were more energetic and accessible. So once again, I went back to the film from the beginning and created a color version. I also expanded the soundtrack with more music and environmental ambience throughout the film. Hopeful that the hard work would pay off, I screened the new version. The film played much better and it was agreed upon that this was going to be the official final cut. After ten long months, the editing had finally ended.

At that point, I think it was fair to say that there was nothing else I could have done to make the film better. I decided while working on the complicated creation of the DVD that I wanted as many people as possible to see the movie, as soon as possible. I uploaded the entire film to Youtube in order to share it with anyone who wanted to see it. I picked the day randomly to upload it and realized soon after that it was Father's Day. I felt it was a sign of good luck and something positive on a day that was difficult for my family.

Sharing the film with the world was a scary experience but a film doesn't exist without an audience. Is it perfect? No, nothing is. However, I committed to doing my best, telling a good story and finishing the task no matter what obstacles I encountered. I honestly feel I accomplished those goals and have grown so much as a filmmaker and a person. I won't let fear stand in my way and I certainly won't let time slip by without appreciating every moment. With the equipment and knowledge I have accumulated over the last two years, I am impatiently preparing for my next film.

Sebastian Howley
September 1st, 2010
Chicago, Illinois

INTRODUCTION

How do you even begin to describe the rollercoaster ride of making a feature film? It doesn't matter if your budget is $100 or $100 million; whether you have made fifty features or this is your first: each film is like starting from scratch. It's the nature of the business that each new project brings about feelings of insecurity and anxiety. This is never more accurate than when you are making your first film.

The title of this book, *One Night to get it right: the making of an Independent film*, points out the common state of mind in which low/no-budget films are made. The pressure to get every shot you need, in a short amount of time, and with limited resources can make you lose focus if you are not prepared. So really, the "making of" in the title of this book is about the film you are going to make as well as the one I already made. Hopefully, this book will make you even more prepared to face the pressure when you have just one night to get it right.

This book was born from the experiences I had making the feature film "One Night." What we lacked in budget, we made up for in an overflowing abundance of energy and a relentlessly positive drive. Because of the nature of our project, this book will focus on how we made something from nothing. When I look back on the past year and half of work it truly feels like we accomplished the impossible. I have been making short films for many years and have written over twenty screenplays but I had never tackled a feature film. Sure there were close calls over the years but the stars never aligned themselves correctly to push a film all the way through.

One word can describe why I had never made the leap to feature films: fear. Sure I can blame finances or any other valid factor but as making "One Night" proved: none of them can really stop you if you don't let them. Fear is the only one. I take filmmaking, and creativity, very seriously. I believe we should challenge ourselves to create unique projects and fill the world with powerful stories that are both personal and well made. Fear had stopped me from moving forward. Fear had stopped me from creating. Once I let go of being afraid, I was off and running and I never looked back.

I wanted to make the perfect first film. I wanted to make a perfect splash into the Hollywood talent pool. I wanted to make the perfect Indie film. Wanting to guarantee something that was perfect was my mistake. Nothing in life is perfect. We make films, these little fake alternate universes, in order to make sense of the real universe. But just like the real universe, nothing is perfect. Every film made has mistakes in it if you look close enough. Every film ever made was produced under all sorts of pressures and demands from the outside world. The one thing that saves a film is a great story.

I have read lists of mistakes from films I have seen multiple times without ever noticing them. After looking for them they pop out so obviously. I usually shrug them off if I loved the movie, simply because of the fact that I loved the movie. The story held my attention or entertained me so well that it didn't matter. On the other hand, films that I greatly disliked I usually noticed mistakes the first time I was watching them. Why? I wasn't into the story. My eyes and ears were wandering away. If I found mistakes or problems they just added fuel to the fire. The point is:

EVERYONE makes mistakes. But after being honest with myself I realized it was just a cover for what was truly stopping me.

I wanted to be appreciated for my talents but I was scared to share my art with the world for fear of rejection. It's that simple. That's all I wanted, but by remaining in suspended animation and not making a feature film, no one had a chance to appreciate my talents and dreams. I had let life roll by without getting in the race because of fear. Life is short. That's my daily mantra now. So one day I woke up and realized my life was slipping away from me. I wasn't getting any younger and I felt like I had let my talents go to waste. I decided I had to make a change. I had to change my mind about something that was deeply grasping my heart. One day, like I said, I let it go. I let go of fear and embraced the uncertainty of life. Meeting my old friend Tony again was the tipping point that set everything in motion.

This leads to my second mantra in life: if you begin a journey, people will join you. If you never start, how can anyone help you? Filmmaking is just a series of decisions from the script, casting, locations, editing, the music: they're all just a series of decisions. The most important decision of course is simply the one to make a film. After I made the decision to take the journey of making a feature film, the path in front of me opened up at every turn. Every time I needed something important, someone appeared before me to help. It's just the way it is. The universe wants to help you but it can't if you don't tell it what you need.

I hope this book takes some of the mystery out of making a film and helps someone overcome the fear that stopped me from creating. Even though I had been making short films for a long time, making a feature was like entering a whole new world. It truly was a journey into the unknown. This book can act as a sort of travel guide for the brave explorers of low/no-budget feature filmmaking.

This book is aimed at the first time director of features as well as the advanced short film director. I don't think making a feature film as a first time project is the way to go. I also don't think people should share their work right from the start. The ease at which people can see completed work nowadays through the Internet is both a blessing and a curse. When you are ready to share your work it can be available to more people and with higher quality with more immediacy than any time in history. Just think, my parents would see newsreels at the movie theater and depended on newspapers as the sole daily source of information. Now anyone with a cell phone can watch video in real time from anywhere in the world. It is truly amazing.

The problem with this is that many people aren't thinking before they create. It is fine to make spoof videos and nonsense for your friends but at some point it should be time to get somewhat serious and personal. The world doesn't need any more celebrity spoof videos. It needs great stories. This is where you come in. My first book on filmmaking put the spotlight on making short films that are more personal and unique. In <u>Independence: capturing the Indie Spirit and making short films that matter,</u> I created a process for disconnecting from the noise of the world and tapping into the sources within you for meaningful stories. That process can be used for feature films as well. By working through that process you can help yourself greatly when it comes time for your first film. The more you work, the more confident you become and this will help you when fear sets in. Because it will. Trust me.

If you have made a bunch of short films and feel like it is time to move into making feature films, this book is for you. No matter how serious you are about making films there are some things you just can't get around. There are certain aspects of filmmaking that are obviously essential to the process. I have broken them down into the usual three categories of pre-production, production and post-production. I have also added sections on finding a film idea, notes about filmmaking, a detailed account of the audition process and what to do after the film is done. Each section is filled with mistakes to avoid, helpful tips, lessons, hints and observations that I collected from my feature filmmaking journey. These entries range from basic processes to creative ideas for overcoming obstacles or how to save yourself from potential trouble. At the end of your journey you will have your own list as well.

The next section covers the progression of posters along with on-set and marketing photos. After that is the last draft of the screenplay of "One Night" before filming began. You can use this to follow along with the film to see how things changed and how they stayed the same. After each scene heading there is a screenshot from the film to give you a sense of location and character. It makes the dry process of reading a screenplay more interesting and visual. I have also included the full technical specifications for producing and editing the film along with a general resource guide.

I truly hope you enjoy this book and my first feature film "One Night." I also hope that after you finish this book you feel empowered to do likewise. As filmmakers, we have the ability to create and share our work with more people and with greater quality than ever before. Make sure you respect that power by telling great stories and enjoying every minute of it. And that is the most important thing of all: enjoy every day. I look forward to hearing about your film as well. My contact information is in the back of the book, so please send me an email when you are finished! But we are getting ahead of ourselves. We have to get your project started first. What are we waiting for? Let's get started by taking the time to ask some very important questions.

FINDING YOUR PROJECT

The following questions will help you begin the journey of making a film. Keep the answers to these questions with you during the entire process in case you ever need to remind yourself why you got involved in this crazy business in the first place.

Beyond the answers to these questions, it is essential that you write down everything during the entire creation of your film. So much time will pass between writing, casting, rehearsal, filming and editing that you will never remember everything. Critical details cannot be left to memory or they will be overlooked and forgotten. It is an important practice, so you can begin by asking yourself these fundamental questions and filling up a few pages in a notebook with the answers.

1) Why are you making a movie?

This can simply be to have fun with your friends or something more long term such as a way to break into a career in filmmaking. This answer should, of course, be in addition to the most important reason: the need to tell a good story.

2) If you could only make one film, is this it?

It is important to find a project that has meaning to you. There is only one chance to make a first impression and you never know what life has in store for you. The closer this film is to your heart the more energy you will have to complete it. Find a story that you absolutely have to tell because you may not get another chance.

3) What do you want to accomplish with this film?

It is important to balance your need to tell a certain story with an understanding of the business side of movies. Balancing your expectations with reality will help you have a better chance of being successful. If you believe your movie is going to play in theaters all over the world and make a hundred million dollars, then you might want to spend some time studying the market. You will probably find that specific goal is unrealistic but it never hurts to aim high. Current Hollywood films hit a wide market after a massive advertisement campaign and then drift away quickly. Indie films work, hopefully, in the opposite way. They start small and gain steam through word of mouth. Set your goals in steps and see how far you can go.

Sometimes I get the feeling that people working in smaller budget Indie films don't want to even think of 'markets' or the DVD as a 'product.' I'm not saying you need to look at it in a cold analytical way as most Hollywood studios do but time should be spent understanding where you want your film to go. A movie doesn't become a movie until an audience sees it. The stress of trying to get the film finished can make it easy to forget this fact. Spend time developing a goal for your film and understand what it takes to reach that objective.

4) Are you ready to make a feature film?

It is very important to ask yourself this question. How many short films have you made? How much time have you spent studying the filmmaking process? Have you studied acting, directing or writing in school? Have you worked as an intern for a production company? If you haven't made a five-minute film that is interesting how can you expect to make a *ninety*-minute film?

5) Making a film is going to take about a year, are you ready for that time commitment?

To do it correctly, even the smallest film might take a year to make from start to finish. It is important to respect the film and let it take the time it needs. If you were baking a cake and only cooked it half the time it is supposed to, how good is that cake going to be? Rushing any aspect of the process does nothing but short change the film, your audience, and everyone who worked on it.

6) What resources do you have access to?

Take time to make a separate list for actors, locations, people with special skills, equipment, and musicians that you know. Most people don't realize how much they have available to them already. Ideas can be born from this list very easily as well as help you in every aspect of making a film. When you are working with a low/no-budget you will need all the help you can get. This can also help you if you get stuck and need a new location or another actor during production. Simply pull out the resource list and you will be prepared to deal with obstacles.

As new people come on board the project you should have them complete a similar resource list and see what they have available also. It never hurts to expand your network and exhaust all opportunities to make your film better.

7) Why make a feature and not a short film?

A feature film demands a certain type of structure and requires a substantial story to be successful. Making a short version of the film can be a good way to find a crew and actors while still focusing on the overall goal of completing a feature length film. Remember: a feature film can take a minimum of a year to complete. Make sure you are ready for that kind of commitment. If your idea can be told satisfactorily in a short film then that's how it should be made.

8) What kind of movies inspire you and why?

If you are unsure of what kind of movie you want to make, it can be helpful to ask yourself some questions about the type of movie that gets you into the movie theater? You can list the movie, the genre and maybe a general theme and see if any patterns appear. This shouldn't be a list of movies you want to copy but more of a reflection of what you are drawn to. The movies you like are saying something that connects to you: what is it?

9) What movies do you dislike and why?

This question follows the previous question's thought process but from a different angle. Certain movies may annoy you, insult you or just bore you to death. Make a list and find out what areas you most want to avoid. Maybe movies with bad dialogue or never ending music make you nuts; it is just as important to know what you don't like as it is to know what you like. When discussing your script with potential actors or crew members it can help to say, "I want to make sure this film is nothing like…" The more detail you can give about what you are trying to accomplish, the clearer it will be for those working to help you achieve it.

10) Are you imitating someone or expressing your own ideas?

Being influenced by other people is impossible to overcome and doesn't have to be entirely. Whenever an artist makes a work of art they are having a direct dialogue with everyone who came before them. Art movements grow and evolve by exploring the boundaries set by the generation before them. It is not entirely wrong to use a previous film as a starting point for your film but it is important that you are using your voice to make the film and not someone else's.

To be honest, if you have nothing to say yourself, then you probably shouldn't be making a film in the first place. Simply put, the more personal and important the story you are trying to tell is, the better you will be in the long run. The amount of work over long periods of time requires a complete *need* to make the film. Simply copying someone else's work won't provide the motivation to overcome the obstacles and stress that filmmaking brings.

NOTES ABOUT FILMMAKING

1

Love what you do. People want to be around good energy and loving what you do generates that endlessly. You will need to rally a group of people to help you and this positive frame of mind will unite them in the right direction. I truly believe that the journey *is* the destination. If you can love what you do every day, then your journey will be worth taking.

The foundation of a great film is a great story. There simply is no way around this. Storytellers have played an important part of society for as long as people could express themselves. Cave paintings highlighted images of important moments and unique people. Folk stories keep cultures connected to the past and inform each new generation of its identity. Filmmaking does the same thing. Regardless of what type of movie you are making: *tell a good story!*

3

Don't be afraid of mistakes. You will make them and so will everyone else. Making your first film is a lot like learning to cook. In a simplified example, say you are learning how to bake an apple pie. You can watch people cook and read cook books but eventually you need to get the ingredients and fire up the oven. The first pie you bake may burn, it may have too much cinnamon, or maybe the apples were not ripe enough. Eventually all these variables will become more manageable and you will be more adept at dealing with them. In its essence, making a film is the same thing. All sorts of nuances may or may not work out but it is impossible to know until you try. Don't let fear talk you out of making something great to share with the world.

4

Find someone you trust to help you. This process is difficult and it will help you to have someone to bounce ideas off of, encourage each other during stressful moments and to help shoulder some of the load. It should be someone you know very well and can count on to be there.

5

Defining the point of view of the film will give it clarity. You cannot make a successful film without a point of view being expressed. Even in an ensemble film, one character usually embodies the complete story arc and unites the multiple plot lines. The point of view tells the audience: this is what is desired and these are the obstacles that are complicating the attainment of those desires. Without it, you won't have a clear emotional drive or a focus in your story.

6

Working within a genre is the best way to get people's attention without stars. Fans of zombie movies will most likely watch whatever zombie movie comes along if it is done well. The average person doesn't care or understand budgets and the intricacies of filmmaking, they simply want to see a good movie. As I mentioned earlier, I wanted to make a more personal film but that potentially limits your audience. I made the film I wanted to make and accept the outcome. I have received quite a few emails from people telling me how much they connected with "One Night" but I know it is never going to be a big theatrical hit. Having a wider audience by working within an established genre will be a big consideration for my next feature. Take time to think about how the type of film you want to make will steer its distribution.

7

Make sure the ideas you are expressing belong to the characters within the film and not yours as the filmmaker. If every character is just a mouthpiece for the writer then you are guaranteed a film full of thin underdeveloped people. The ideas have to come from the characters organically and not be force-fed by the writer. Let each character speak for themselves, so there are a variety of unique personalities. If you cover the names of the characters in your script and can't tell the difference in how they speak, then it means they don't have individual voices.

8

Think visually. Early drafts are meant to be over-written but as you go through the rewriting process it is important to simplify and to think visually. Filmmaking, in its most basic terms, is the telling of a transformative story through visual information.

It is far more interesting to see a man lay flowers on a grave then slowly walk in the snow to a small bar that's decorated for Christmas, sit down alone and have his usual drink placed in front of him without ordering than have the same man have a phone conversation telling someone he misses his wife and is drinking too much because of it. Same information but it is told in a profoundly different way. Film is a visual art. Think visually and you will establish a strong foundation in which to tell your story.

9

It is important to add movement to activate scenes as well. Too many passive scenes of talking can make a movie stagnate and dull. Always give the actors something to do in a scene. It should be simple as to not distract but enough to allow them to keep active. You could have two people just sitting in a kitchen having a conversation, but it would be better to have one sitting and the other cooking. This could add a level of conflict between the two if the person cooking dinner feels like a servant or maybe add humor if the person is a terrible cook and struggles to make a simple meal. It doesn't have to be over-the-top but simple actions can activate a scene while reinforcing the underlying subtext of the script.

Structure is vital to a successful film. Pacing and the progress towards a catharsis can only be managed by paying close attention to the structure of the screenplay. Just writing a bunch of scenes and hoping they add up to something won't cut it. When editing the film you may find arbitrary shots within a scene to use but the organization of the scenes overall is never random. Scenes without purpose to the overall story will derail your audience's attention and grind your story momentum to a halt.

It is highly debated how exact the structure of a film needs to be but regardless, you must pay close attention to it. I suggest reading as many screenplay writing books as you can or taking a course and making up your mind for yourself. There are several highly recommended examples in the resource guide in the back of this book to help you craft a successful screenplay.

11

In general, films are visual stories showing the physical and emotional transformation of a character. I mention several times in this book the critical need to visually tell your story to illustrate how vital it is to a successful film. It is worth repeating, as this is one of the most ignored aspects of filmmaking. I constantly see films nowadays that come across as ninety-minute sitcoms. You should be able to turn off the sound and still be able to understand almost everything about a film. I suggest taking time to watch some silent films in order to understand the power and technique of visual storytelling. Just watch Charlie Chaplin's film "The Kid" and you will see how scenes can be either funny or dramatic without a single word being spoken. I'm not saying you can't have dialogue but your film will become more powerful and more accessible if you build the story visually.

When you have a completed script, make a list of the scenes, a brief description, the locations and the scene lengths. It will allow you to see if you have enough variation in your story and if you have possibly bitten off more than you can chew. If you know you are working with a small budget and after making your list you have thirty locations and forty-five actors that have lines you might want to rethink your script. Each rewrite of your script should be guided by the sobering fact that what you are writing is actually going to have to be filmed.

13

The lead character in a film needs to move the action and not the other way around. A passive lead in a film takes away the momentum that needs to build as it moves towards a resolution.

The basic theme of all stories is change. A story should be full of turning points, transformation and the moving through a unique experience. You can break it down in a very basic way as either a character's world is turned upside down and it has to be restored or a character has an unsatisfying life and rises to the challenge of finding happiness.

It is important to work with emotional variations as well as length and the physical location of the scenes. Contrasting emotional tones from scene to scene allow for a greater impact over the course of a film. Too many scenes of the same length and emotional tone will make people disengage from the characters and the story.

Think of the ocean when it comes to varying scene structure. As the tide comes in, it may rush the shores with great power or gently roll in splashing against your feet. Then as it recedes the shores are uncovered allowing birds or crabs to calmly walk around freely for a few moments. The waves come back, covering over the shore and creating a completely different environment and feeling. It's a simple analogy but an important one. Variation in tone and scene length will keep your audience with you for the ride.

15

A movie promises a resolution based on the setting up of a character and their particular struggle. The most important aspect of making a successful film is to deliver on the promise made by the set-up. Imagine a joke being told and then the release of energy in the form of laughter at the revealing of the punch line. The longer and more complicated the set-up is, the more we expect the joke to deliver. The set-up must give us the pieces we need emotionally at the conclusion and the conclusion must justify the journey the audience went on to get there.

PRE-PRODUCTION

1

Filmmaking is a privilege and you should always push yourself to do your best by working at your highest level. If you don't want to sacrifice the required time to it then it will show. Always do your best. That way, you will live a life without regrets and have a body of work that is built on integrity and purpose.

2

Whether you write the script yourself or have a writing partner, never base the script on source material that you don't own the rights to. I have met a bunch of people over the years that have spent countless hours, weeks, and months working on something that can't actually make. If you don't own it, don't write it.

If you have written something already like this, don't throw it away. Take the script and stash it away for later. If your first film is a big hit maybe you will one day be in the position to work with other people's material and you will be all set. If you are about to sit down and write the sequel to Pulp Fiction, please stop. Unless you want to do it as a writing challenge or practice, that's fine but time is better spent working on your own ideas.

3

The more you prepare in pre-production the better off you will be for the rest of the journey. At this point in the project you have to start making some big decisions. One of the biggest obstacles in Independent filmmaking is wading through the dark waters of legal and business structures. The best way to do this is to talk to a lawyer and do research on your business options. You have to decide whether you want to create a company and continue to make films or whether you want to create a business entity just for this one film.

You also need to decide how you will raise money. Even using words like "donate" and "invest" carry legal implications and you have to be very careful. Creating a business structure like a Limited Liability Company (LLC) is an option that most people do, including myself. There are no easy answers when it comes to this subject so the more research you do the better. I always work under the assumption that the project I am creating could be successful so it is best to be prepared. If you don't take the steps to cover your bases you could see the benefits of your hard work be compromised or lost altogether.

4

Get everything in writing. Every commitment or agreement between you and an actor or a location or anything related to the film, needs to be in writing. Always cover your bases.
There some great sample contract resources online and this is another area a lawyer can help you with.

Get everything in writing!

5

For the auditions I prepared three scenes and three monologues from the script. I got a blog started to use just for the auditions and posted complete character descriptions, audition locations, times and instructions. We held scheduled auditions on a Saturday and then we had open auditions on Sunday. On the blog, I posted all the available times for Saturday and as they got taken I just updated the entry so people had real time information.

6

The driving force of a low/no-budget film is the cast. A film is brought to life and filled with the personality of its characters. Casting is absolutely essential to a small film's success. The smaller the film the more focus that will be placed on individual performances as opposed to elaborate set pieces, special effects or exotic locations.

7

If you are lucky enough to have talented friends then God bless you, but most people don't. Your friends may want to help but remember that acting, in general, takes training and dedication. Acting on film is difficult even for trained actors. In fact, if the actors are heavily experienced in theater they may have a difficult time translating their skills to film as they are completely different forms of expression. A poorly cast film can ruin its chances regardless if you have the best script ever written.

8

Remember casting is a two way street. You will be judged during the audition process as well. Be professional, be prepared and stay on schedule.

During the audition process, I had the people running the sign-in table take notes on the actors. People can be their perfect self in the audition room but act like a maniac or a jerk beforehand. It is worth knowing this, trust me. If they were on-time and treated others with respect are pieces of information that can help you get to know the actors better. Whoever runs the sign-in process should keep their eyes and ears open the whole time.

Running a smooth audition will build confidence in the people you are hoping to work with. First impressions are important when beginning a project that demands as much as making a film does. If they think you aren't prepared or it appears that you don't know what you are doing, then you will be sunk before you even set sail.

For instance, if you hold auditions make it very clear whether your film will be open to SAG/Union actors. This makes a huge difference and will waste a lot of people's time if you are not hiring union actors for budgetary reasons and some show up. Following this section I have included all of the postings and emails I used in casting " One Night." Hopefully, they can help you create an efficient and effective casting experience.

10

In order to review each person's audition in the most thorough way, I suggest videotaping them. This will allow you to go back and refresh your memory about an actor's personality and voice. Before they begin, have each actor state their name and the role they are reading for directly into the camera. Some people actually have the actors write their name out on a piece of paper and hold it as a sort of slate. Whatever you decide, have them give their name as it will help you identify them in case their headshot gets lost.

When giving friends a part in the film, there may be a chance that they may not appreciate how important their performance is to the film. Actors who are cast on the other hand should potentially feel as though they earned the part and bring more energy and focus to it. Actors who audition also have a career they will want to promote and after the movie is done, they will have more incentive to get the word out. Think long and hard about giving roles away as opposed to holding auditions.

You should have an emergency contact sheet for every person that will be on the set. Once the film is cast, get an accordion folder and place their headshot and emergency contact information sheet in it.

13

Once the script is locked down and the entire cast is set, you should have a read-through. Get everyone together and on the same page-literally and figuratively. Planning this read through will introduce you to the joy of scheduling. You will become acquainted with the struggle of getting everyone in one place at one time very quickly. This will be the perfect time to get everyone's schedule synched up and in line for rehearsing.

Don't think you can just hand out scripts and then show up some day in the future and make it happen. As with everything in life, you will get out of this project what you put in to it. Spend time listening to the flow of the dialogue, the pacing of the scenes and the overall tone. Notice how your actor's relate to each other or how they don't. Spend the time in pre-production to fix any problems related to the script or the actors.

Videotape, photograph and record the audio of every rehearsal. Reviewing how the script reads can help you hear problem areas or maybe pick up nuances you hadn't thought of. No matter how many times you have read the script, it will come alive in so many different ways when read by the actors. When you are finished with the film, you can use parts of this along with their audition tape in a 'behind the scenes' video for the DVD's extra features.

As you review the rehearsed scenes make some notes on what lines of dialogue and thematic moments would make a great trailer. It is never too early to begin to think of how this film will be introduced to the world. Watch as many trailers as you can online and get an idea of how they are put together.

Direct open communication is the backbone of any successful organization. The only way to make a group run effectively is through clearly letting people know what they need to do and when they need to do it. From the moment you post the audition notices to the day you hand the cast their copy of the DVD, you need to clearly communicate with your cast and crew.

Once the cast has gathered for the first time, you need to bottle that energy and keep it fresh and positive. Nothing will deflate the potential of a project than leaving a cast and crew wondering what is going on.

Get a lock-box for the set. As actors arrive you can place everyone's valuables and cell phones in the box. This box should be kept locked in a secure place out of view. After changing into wardrobe, it will allow people to know exactly where their valuables are during filming. Also, it will allow you to make sure everyone's cell phones are turned off and won't ruin a shot by accidentally ringing in the middle of a take.

Buy a rolling hanging rack to organize wardrobe on the set. It will allow you to have the actors' costumes ready to go when they arrive and then a place for their street clothes to be in an organized way during filming. The less clutter on the set the better. The rolling racks are inexpensive, lightweight and incredibly handy. You can also throw a heavy sheet over them and use it for sound dampening when needed.

18

After you have had several table readings of the script and you feel that the text is ready to be locked down, try getting as much work done on the sets as you can. If you have access to any locations before filming, rehearse scenes there. The actors can get a feel for the environment and the crew will know exactly how much room they have to work with.

Before filming in any location you should visit the space with the cinematographer and sound technician to map out issues. We went into a few locations cold and it added to the stress of filming each time. We didn't have access beforehand so it was out of our control and that can make things much more difficult on yourself. With low/no-budget films, you don't always have the luxury of spending time in a location before you show up to film. If you can, it is well worth it. Identifying power sources, lighting or sound issues, and the availability of bathrooms among other things will give you a better chance of working smoothly in each location.

Find out in advance if permits or special insurance is needed for any location you are using. If you search "filming insurance" on the internet, you will come across quite a few types. The basic insurance covers damage to property but not to people. It will be based on type of project, stunts involved, filming at heights, use of guns etc. The insurance will run for a very specific time period so if you do purchase it, make sure you film during that time period or you will need to purchase it again.

Never introduce new equipment when you are filming. If there is a piece of gear that will be new to anyone, pre-production is the time to experiment with it and understand its capabilities.

We used a lens adaptor that was new to the cinematographer and the first day of filming it caused problems. The adaptor's vibration caused picture distortion and we didn't have the simple fix the first day. Consequently we had some shots that were usable and others that needed a lot of time in post-production to be fixed. It only affected one day of filming but as far as I am concerned there should be no surprises when you get to the set. Pre-production is the time to work out any issues while filming rehearsals.

During pre-production get creative when you can't afford equipment or set pieces. Anything you can't borrow or buy can be made for much cheaper. The table rail unit we used was perfectly reliable and easy to use. PVC tubing was mounted onto a piece of pressboard and then placed on a table or the ground to deliver even tracking shots.

Simple camera movement adds another level of sophistication to your film and can increase the creative possibilities of a shot. Too many static tripod shots or unsteady handheld shots can ruin your film by either being lifeless or distracting by uncontrolled movement.

I suggest keeping a dated journal from the moment you decide to make the film until it is all done. The bulk of this book came from the notes I made during the process of making the film. One of the benefits is simply to keep track of what you are doing. I will mention it several times in this book but everything you do should be put in writing. Not only in the contractual side of things but also just your goals and actions.

After the filming is finished and you are ready to market the film you will never remember who did what when. From these notes you can develop a timeline and also sort through what it took to make the film. Every film has a story behind how it was made. Indie films, in particular, usually have some very entertaining adventures during production. It is important to be able to convey exactly what it took for you to get the film made. I can guarantee you will never remember the details after the dust settles. You will need all the help you can in trying to piece together what you accomplished or, God forbid, where things went wrong. It will also serve as a way to remind you that even small films rely on a number of people helping. When your film is finished, you will be able to go back and know exactly who to thank.

There are some basic tools for the set that should be purchased before filming starts. A fire extinguisher and an advanced first aid kit should be on the set at all times. At the start of filming they should be put in an accessible place and everyone should be made aware of where they are.

Instant coffee, chocolate covered espresso beans and non-perishable items like bottled water, power bars and trail mix should be ready to go on day one of filming. Food that can spoil should only be bought on a day-to-day basis. Even if you are operating on a "no-budget" type film shoot, the cast and crew has to be fed. If you feed people at least they are receiving something they can immediately enjoy during the process. People obviously don't work well with low energy, so feeding people is mandatory.

I personally believe that using guns is a bad idea. I think it is a cheap way to create drama and in the end not very creative. I have known people who used guns in projects before and I have heard of people using unloaded real guns as well. Even if they were unloaded it is stupid and probably illegal.

Safety of the cast and crew is the number one concern while making a movie. Nothing comes above that at any time. Guns are just asking for trouble. Most likely if you are working in the low/no-budget world, no one knows you are making your movie. So that means neighbors, passer-bys and the police don't know that the person they just saw run by their window with a gun is acting in a movie. It may seem obvious to you but it may not be to them. My advice is to leave the guns to studio films that have the resources and expertise to deal with them.

Once the script is locked down you can prepare the shooting schedule. There are so many variables to scheduling a film that it is impossible to get into details here but there are some general points that will help. The first thing you need to do is number the scenes/shots in the script. The basic system simply sets a number for the scene and is then followed by a shot number. Once deciding on a system you need to stick with it and continue through the entire production. These numbers will allow you to keep track of every required shot, as well as to synch audio to the video files in post-production. For example, for the third shot in scene two you would call it "2.3" in your script.

A sample of a shooting script would look like this:

2.0 INT. EDDIE'S APARTMENT-DAY

Eddie lies on the floor.

A knock at the door.

Eddie opens his eyes.

2.1 He sits up.

> NEIGHBOR (O.S.)
> Eddie, quit daydreaming and open
> the door.

2.2 Eddie stands, walks to the door and
opens it.

2.3 A young man (NEIGHBOR) stands in the
     doorway, holds a globe.

> NEIGHBOR (CONT'D)
> I think this belongs to you.

2.4 Eddie and the neighbor sit on the
     ground with the globe between them.

I broke the script down into pieces so it was easier to manage. I made a packet for every single scene in the film. The first page of the packet had all the necessary information needed for filming. This way when I was preparing for the next day all I had to do was check each packet. The top of the first page had the scene number, then the filming date and time, cast needed and their start times, location information (address, parking info etc.) and prop list.

This is the script I worked off of when filming each scene. I always had the complete script within reach but it is easier to work off of just a few pages than off of ninety. This scene breakdown can be emailed to everyone involved in that days filming. There are many types of software designed just for film scheduling and you can decide which one works for you. But you have to decide on some system, as working without a written organized schedule is not an option.

One item worth buying is a small folding table. They are available at lots of stores and are usually four to six feet long and can be folded in half for storing or transporting easily. It can be used as a prop table during set-up at each location. From the front page of your daily scene breakdown you have a prop list and can tape it to the table. All the items can be checked in and out during the day. It can be very easy to lose or damage props or wardrobe and you will have enough to worry about already.

We had an incident with the main character, Eddie, and his hat. In an attempt to pinch pennies, I only bought one hat for him to wear which was not a great idea. The hat was put down on the kitchen table during a break in the apartment we were filming in and it was placed on a spill. It stained the hat and we had no way of replacing it late at night. I should have been prepared and I wasn't. I pride myself in always thinking ahead but this slipped through the cracks. In one scene, when the four main characters come back to the apartment and sit on the couch together you can notice the stain on the right side of his hat. I bought a replacement so that was the only place it made it into the movie but that was a moment of frustration for me. I should have bought a second hat and it was a reminder to have a place for props/wardrobe to be placed safely.

It is important to take each scene on its own terms because it is very easy to get overwhelmed by the challenge of filming an entire script. If you can concentrate on one scene, one step at a time, you can take control of what could easily get out of hand.

A good way to do this is to understand the essence of each scene. Just as it is important to know what your film is about, it is important to understand the function of each scene. You can't build a completely coherent film without having a clear purpose for every scene.

When you are making your scene breakdown packets make an extra section for yourself that describes exactly what the scene is about and how it relates to the film. This basic purpose will help you keep focused and remind you exactly what you need at that moment.

Never be afraid to ask people for help. People will almost always be willing to help you for free. Locations, props, or almost anything can be found if you look. Some people I have worked with are afraid to knock on doors or just walk into a store and ask for the use of their location. Honestly, the average person doesn't have the knowledge of what it takes to make a movie and won't care if yours is low/no-budget. That concept only matters to filmmakers not to normal people. Normal people are usually happy to be included in something that is exciting and different.

No one bothered us in any way when we were filming. A couple of times people stopped to watch but no one ruined a shot or disrupted us at all. Making a movie is exciting to people and unusual so build on that and ask people for help. We had every location we needed and more by simply asking. Treat people and their property with respect and you will have opportunities open to you: all you need to do is ask.

You can make postcards at any time to help get the word out. If you attract attention from people while filming, hand them a postcard and tell them to keep an eye out for your film. It's never too early to spread the word.

31

I think it is essential that all directors take some sort of acting class. You can audit a course at a community college or find some local theater that offers classes. I had the advantage of having worked as an actor for some years so I was able to bring that experience to the set. Being able to communicate with the actors in terms that made sense to them allowed for a set without conflict. I also was able to understand exactly what is reasonable to ask of them and what they need in order to perform in certain situations. Understanding the acting process firsthand is something I believe will go a long way to helping you build a better knowledge of an essential component of the filmmaking process.

Certain jobs on the set are open to anyone who is nice enough to help. Other jobs truly need to be handled by someone with specific experience. It is very easy to have too much of a good thing on a film set. Too few people helping and you may not be prepared to handle the workload. Too many people and you then have extra mouths to feed, extra noise during filming and people possibly interrupting shots.

We maintained the smallest crew you can physically have and we barely made it. It is important not to forget that equipment doesn't move itself. If you have to strike the set everyday after filming people will be tired and it helps to have fresh bodies to lend a hand. It takes some time to find the right balance. It is very common to have ten people say they will be there and only one show up. If you do make some short films leading up to your feature you can begin to find responsible people then.

You should be able to write out the essence of the film in one sentence, a paragraph and then a whole page. If you are unable to write a simple sentence conveying the basic plot line of the film then it's possible that you don't really know what the film is about. A simple one-line description gives you a lot of vital information that dictates the course of the entire film. This will also help any time someone asks about your movie; you will have an interesting and concise way to describe it to them.

The less people on the set the better. The first few days you may have friends who offer their help. However, they may be more curious than competent when it comes to actually helping you. Remember every person on the set needs to eat, take bathroom breaks, and will potentially make noise. Make sure if you invite people to help, they are there for a reason and understand what is expected of them.

If people volunteer to be extras they have to understand they will need to basically sit around for hours. Making a movie always sounds interesting from a distance but after five hours of sitting in a hot stuffy room it becomes a lot less exciting. You can run into significant continuity problems if filming runs over into a second day and the background actors can't make it. If you have already filmed the master shot with them then you either have to start from scratch or deal with extras disappearing from shot to shot.

Once again, clearly communicate the hours people are needed and what is expected of them so you can avoid tension on the set and continuity problems from extras.

Often, low/no-budget films will rely on heavy dialogue in limited locations in place of costlier action scenes, special effects or multiple locations. Besides the danger that the end result will be visually uninteresting, there are some serious challenges in this filming approach.

Unless you are lucky enough to have a location that can be locked down, you are going to run into sound issues. If you have scenes that are mainly relying on dialogue, make sure the location can accommodate the prolonged stretches of quiet needed to film.

AUDITION MATERIALS

As I mentioned earlier, I think it is important to go into more detail about the audition process. We were able to find great actors and a cinematographer through hard work and some great luck. The success of our auditions came from being prepared and from keeping people informed as much as possible each step of the way.

One thing you will notice after reading the audition materials and then watching the movie is how completely different the character of Veronica end up. She evolved into a much more interesting role based on the actresses' input and the realization that I had under-written the part. It is vital to trust your intuition and know when to make a change. Originally, the character of Max and Veronica were dating but it hit me during rehearsals that there needed to be some sort of underlying conflict between the group. I decided that instead of already being a couple, Max and Veronica would be going out on their first date on the night of the film. This created a nice contrast to the characters of Eddie and Nina who are ex's seeing each other for the first time since they broke up. When the night begins everyone puts up a good front but slowly the truth of how lost they all are in life makes its way to the surface. This was exactly the underlying tension and narrative energy the story needed.

INITIAL ONLINE POSTING

Auditions are being held on Saturday May 23rd and Sunday 24th for the feature film "**_One Night_**."

The film follows two couples through the course of one night as they wander through the city of Chicago. As the world appears to be falling apart around them, each character must come to terms with what is truly important in life.

The film centers on the character of Eddie as he is evicted from his apartment and then bumps into his ex-fiancé. This chaotic night could be his one chance to reconnect with the love of his life. Funny, poetic and emotional, the film aims to follow in the footsteps of other great Indie favorites such as Kicking and Screaming (1995), Bottle Rocket, Before Sunrise, Garden State, and Stranger Than Paradise.

"**_One Night_**" will be filmed on High Definition Digital Video. We are planning DVD sales on Amazon and iTunes and rentals through Netflix.

We are looking for all ethnic types as we want as diverse a cast as we can have. We are casting for the following three characters:

1) **EDDIE**: script age 30 (actor ages 27-33) A broken-hearted writer, Eddie is a good soul who is lost in life. Rambunctious, eager to run head first into schemes and daydreams, impetuous and impossibly charming. His love for Nina has not died since they split up, leaving him with a massive novel about their relationship that just gets longer and longer. Eddie could spend all day passionately discussing

UFOs, conspiracies theories, comics, Godzilla movies, art and philosophy, but trying to hold down a job, well that is another story.

2) **NINA**: *script age 30 (actor ages 27-33) A stylish, artistic, smart and independent spirit. She doesn't need anyone's permission to live her life and is not intimidated by anyone. However, her cool, strong exterior hides an insecure and self-conscious woman who would rather make art for herself than do commercial graphic design for companies. Her great style (retro hip with a touch of rockabilly) has her labeled as "the cool hip girl" by the older staid people in her workplace. She broke Eddie's heart but hers hasn't healed either, leaving her to fill her life with work which has left her lonely in the city.*

3) **VERONICA**: *script age 22 (actor ages 20-25) Veronica is a photographer who is coming to terms with life after college. She is dating Max, a musician, and is in the midst of a vow of silence, which she won't break until she solved her artistic crisis. She is naive and a bit immature. She gets bored easily and often wanders off causing Max to track her down. She is moody and sensitive but only because she so sincerely wants to find her place in this world. Eddie and her are like oil and water, as she feels Max is too eager to follow around Eddie on some pointless scheme. She finds solace in the crowded dance floor of the club her brother DJs at.*

4) MAX. *The part of Max has been cast.*

FILMING SPECIFICS

*This is a non-union, non-SAG film.

*The filming of this feature will take place between July 6th through the 13th.

*The filming will be mainly night shoots.

TO AUDITION:

The audition will consist of a cold reading and possibly the reading of a monologue. The monologue does not need to be memorized, just be familiar with it in case you are asked to read it. It will be provided before the audition.

Follow these steps to audition for the film:

1) Email your headshot and resume to [email address}

2) We will be auditioning from 11-4 on Saturday (23rd) in five minute time slots with a break from 1:00 to 1:30 for lunch.

Please check the blog posting "Audition Schedule" for open times and specify in your email your preferred audition time.

State which character you are auditioning for and the monologue for that character will be emailed with the confirmation of your audition time.

3) On Sunday (24th) from 10:00 to 12:00 and 12:30 to 3:00 we will be auditioning with open times. First come first served.

4) Callbacks will be determined after auditions are complete.

If you are unable to attend these auditions, please email your headshot and resume to us and we will still consider you.

{If you can't attend and want to go the extra mile, record a basic video of your reading of the monologue provided and upload it to Youtube, Vimeo or any other video uploading site and email us the URL to the video along with your headshot and resume.}

PLEASE do this in one email not two separate ones. PLEASE do not send the video as a file attachment, just send the URL once it is posted.

COMPENSATION:

*All actors will receive a DVD copy and any related materials released with the film (soundtrack CD, book, posters, etc.)

*There will be monetary compensation to be determined after casting for travel.

* Meals will be provided during rehearsals, meetings and filming.

This film is being made by people who love making movies. We want to make a profitable film but one that speaks deeply to those involved in the production as well as those watching the end results.

This will be a stripped-down, bare-bones production that needs performers that love the craft of acting and are not drowning in a sea of prima-donna ego. This film shoot will be hard work but we truly believe we have a great script that will serve as a strong foundation for a memorable film.

We own all the equipment we need in order to make this film, from start to finish, so there are no obstacles to getting the project completed. This is not one of those films that disappears after the shooting is wrapped. We plan to have a large rollout through local and national media and will not rest until the film is out in the world.

We look forward to hearing from you.

We plan on working steadily after this film so headshots and resumes will be kept on file for future projects.

If you have any questions about the auditions or the film please contact us at {email address}

MONOLOGUES

EDDIE

Every superpower is just some form of perverted narcissism. All of them except Superman's indestructibility. He had all them together. That's smart. You're supposed to have super powers to help the world. Most of them are just selfish. All of them are just selfish, actually. Flying. Flying is the worst. Everyone wants to fly. You can fly in a plane or a helicopter or a hang glider, flying is redundant. X-ray vision makes no sense also. So you can see through something? What if you get shot? A lot of help you'd be. And forget about invisibility. That's the worst of them all. You give ten guys invisibility and they would be hanging out in some dressing room at the mall or in a women's locker room somewhere. Not one of them would try to save the world. See that's why female super heroes are practical. Wonder woman's jet was invisible not her. Stealth, now that's smart and her bullet proof wrist bracelets. She could get the job done. If I had to choose one? Honestly? Invisibility.

VERONICA

I lied to you. I wasn't mad at you for ruining my pictures. I mean I was mad but I was upset with myself about my photos. I hated them. They were garbage. You did what I didn't have the heart to do, and that was to get rid of them. I just wasn't ready to admit that. However, the next time you come over and you see a sign on the bathroom door or any door that says 'do not enter.' Please do me the favor and do not enter. Ok?

NINA

You know if you are serious about trying to be a part of my life and for us to start over again, it would be nice if you had both a place to live and a job. Like a normal person. We aren't kids anymore Eddie. Now you have to actually mentally grow up and take responsibility for yourself. I like you. I miss you. But since the last time we saw each other you haven't really moved forward very much have you? When are you going to take charge of your life? When? Are you still blaming me for where you are in life? Because if you are then there is no hope for us to even be friends. Let alone whatever else is cooking up in that brain of yours. If you can't let go of the past Eddie there's no hope for a future. Not for yourself, and definitely not for us.

FOLLOW-UP EMAIL

We hope this email finds everyone doing well. We want to thank everyone for the immediate and overwhelming response. We filled the weekend's audition times in just hours, forcing us to take the posting down. In fact it was the only place we even put the job posting. Clearly, it was all we needed.

We are very excited about the response because of the high level of talent and diversity we received. This email will hopefully give everyone a clearer picture of the characters for which you will be auditioning and the overall project itself. Attached to this email is the scene(s) for the character(s) you will be reading for.

Because the response has been so overwhelming, we want to provide the sides as early as possible so that the auditions themselves run smoothly. This will also set up the day to run quickly and efficiently. This extra time will also allow for any and all questions you have to be answered, giving all of you a confident foundation to show us the best well-developed reading you can.

Neither the sides nor the monologues need to be memorized, just be comfortable with them. The monologue will only be read if time allows or during a callback.

STORY/FILM BACKGROUND

The backbone of this film is a response to the world we have all found ourselves in. The fragility of the world economy, the growing paranoia and isolation of a world based on technology, and the violent reactions to the potential chaos in the world are all weighing on the minds and hearts of people. It would be easy to crawl up in a little ball and hide but these characters don't.

As a writer, I couldn't help but feel a need to address all the conflicts we are going through emotionally and financially. When businesses close, jobs are lost and the world changes quickly we must ask ourselves: what is truly important in my life? That is where these characters find themselves one night.

I always try to approach life with a sense of humor. So even amid all these fears and growing instability there has to be room to enjoy simple things in life. Without laughter and love, life has little joy. I have tried to develop a story and group of characters that embody these ideas. The films mentioned in the audition posting on the blog show fairly well the tone of the film we are going for.

If you are cast in this film there will be room to add yourself to the role, allowing for a deeper personal performance. I want everyone involved in this project to feel they are proud of the film in general and their work within it. The following character breakdowns are from the basic structure of the script and will grow in complexity when the film is cast.

CHARACTER RELATIONSHIPS

EDDIE AND MAX

Eddie and Max are close friends and have been for a long time. They are supportive of each other's work and are not competitive. They both want the other to achieve success. They have a great sense of humor with each other. They can spend hours drinking coffee and discussing existential questions, pop culture, and how to navigate the perilous world of relationships. Eddie and Max have been friends long enough for Max to get beyond Eddie's schemes and impulsiveness.

EDDIE AND NINA

Eddie and Nina have known each other since they were kids. Friends for some time they eventually drifted apart. In college they began dating and stayed together for seven years. Eddie's inability to make the transition to being a 'grown-up' created a divide between them.

Eddie and Nina haven't spoken in over a year since they broke up. When they meet on this night enough time has passed to calm their emotions but the feelings linger just under the surface. As with someone who knows you like the back of their hand, it only takes a few words to make you either laugh in hysterics or scream in frustration. Nina has done the improving and Eddie has done the floundering since the break-up. Still they are in some ways emotionally in the same place. The instability of the world around them adds to the urgency in being with the person you love. The question is whether or not they are truly made for each other.

MAX AND VERONICA

Max met Veronica when she was one of his guitar students. She is much younger than him and it often shows. She may be serious about becoming a good photographer but she is too unsure of herself to make the steps towards her goal. It is easier for her to lose herself in music, wander aimlessly or just sit by the lake and listen to the waves.

Max's life is more structured compared to hers but he is just as lost. The difference is the fact that he is older and understands that you can only improve yourself through hard work and not by surrendering to the obstacles.

EDDIE'S MONOLOGUE

Eddie's monologue occurs early in the film and is a non-sequitor. It is a typical conversation between Eddie and Max in which Eddie carries on about some random thought that he is focused on. Eddie speaks with conviction and passion but often about subjects or ideas he hasn't necessarily thought out completely. In this monologue he is as much convincing himself as he is Max of some belief.

NINA'S MONOLOGUE

Nina's monologue takes place in the middle of the film during one of the first conversations Nina and Eddie have after seeing each other. Nina begins to have second thoughts about spending the night wandering around the city with Eddie as it appears he has not changed. In fact in many ways he has gone backwards. Instead of playing it safe she decided to tell him very directly how she feels about him and his place in the world.

VERONICA'S MONOLOGUE

Veronica's monologue takes place at the end of the film. All four of them have separated and regrouped after realizing what they mean to each other. Deep down Veronica and Eddie are similar but both are in denial of seeing themselves reflected in someone who is immature. Veronica has broken her vow of silence and tells Eddie the truth about what happened to her photos.

I hope this email creates a clearer picture of the film and the individual characters. I hope it makes your audition more developed and confident. Please let us know if there is anything else you need to know in order to help you succeed next Saturday or Sunday.

FINAL EMAIL

This email will give some last minute instructions in hopes of making this weekend an efficient and satisfying process.

We have tried to provide clear instructions on scheduling an audition time, providing sides and monologues with plenty of time to become familiar with them and now we are clarifying the process of the audition itself. If you have any questions please do so by Friday evening at 9:00 p. m., as that is the last time email questions will be answered.

Listed below is a simple check-list you can print and use to prepare for your audition.

1) Please bring your headshot and resume with you to the audition. (If you don't have headshots, at least type up a resume so we can have something on file when reviewing the auditions.)

2) Print the attached file, complete it and bring it to the audition to expedite the check-in process. Staple this page to the back of your headshot.

3) If you have a Saturday audition please come a few minutes early and be ready when your time is called. If you are late there is no way to fit you back into the audition schedule as we are booked straight through to the end. There is a show in the theater space at night and we must be out exactly on time.

4) If you have a Sunday audition, make sure you come at a time when you have some flexibility. Please be patient and prepared.

5) As with any audition, you may not read through the entire scene. Do your best to dive right into it and show us what you have.

6) Remember this is an audition for a film and not a play. Gestures, vocal volume and intensity should be controlled and minimal. The emotional energy you build up during your 'moment before' should be channeled through your eyes and face. It should be subtle and simple. The performance is personal; it's for the camera and not the back of the house.

7) With the great response we got, most likely, time will allow for just the scene to be read through. Spend more time with this than the monologue.

We look forward to meeting all of you and we hope everyone has a great time reading this weekend.

Please let us know if you have any questions by 9:00 p.m. Friday evening as no questions will be answered after that time.

Good luck!

<u>PRODUCTION</u>

1

When you set your schedule, stick to it. Unless something unseen stops you from following the schedule, you need to keep your word. You will lose the confidence of the cast and crew if you can't keep your word when it comes to planning the basic filming schedule. Most likely everyone in your cast and crew will have day jobs, so juggling schedules and taking time off may not be easy.

During our filming the flu spread through the cast and crew and made filming impossible for a short time. We lost three days of work but there was nothing we could do. One of the nights of filming was going to be a party scene that involved a location with limited availability and lots of extras. We managed to get the location for another night but it was not in enough time to fill the place with people again. Instead of it being a crowded crazy party I simply rewrote the tone of the scene. We managed to get a few people to show up so it wasn't completely empty. The scene still works and it adds an awkward and humorous angle as they show up uninvited to a birthday party that is a ghost town. We were able to think on our feet and adapt to the new situation while maintaining the narrative integrity of the scene.

2

When you make the schedule, plan the simplest set up and shot first. Let your first day be easy and a way to help get everyone on the same page with a temporary sense of accomplishment. Hopefully you will already have filmed some rehearsals, visited the location prior to filming and worked the scene with the actors thoroughly. All this preparation will pay off when filming finally begins and it is for real. Starting off with an easy shot and an easy scene will get the film moving forward in a positive direction.

It is easy to get into the technical aspects when filming and forget that your actors are living breathing beings. Monitoring your actors' energy levels will help support a successful shoot. It doesn't mean you have to baby the actors but no one likes to be treated like an inanimate object. Film sets get very warm and the air gets stale quickly. Between the heat from the lights and the fact that the air conditioning is turned off for sound quality, a set can be an ugly place if you add negative energy to the equation.

This all comes back to the importance of everyone being prepared before showing up on the set. The creation of a film is a progression of actions. The end result is an accumulation of decisions and preparation that happen every step of the way. The rehearsals you have prior to filming will gauge how prepared your actors are and the filming process will then show up in the editing room.

If you are filming with a camera that uses MiniDV tapes you need to make sure you have established a safe place for them. As soon as you take a full tape out of the camera, make sure to slide over the button that prevents recording. Obviously protecting your work is a top priority on the set. A small lock box similar to the one for valuables can be used to keep the tapes away from liquid, heat, or magnets.

If you are using a hard drive recorder for video as well as a digital recorder for audio, these files should be backed-up on set immediately to an external hard drive. If you dump down the video and/or audio to a laptop then back it up right away. Don't wait for later to do that. The digital world we live in is fragile and a crashed hard drive can ruin a lot of hard work. Every step of the way in making a film will involve covering your bases and protecting your work. Never wait for later to save and back up your work.

6

Wardrobe for actors should be kept on the hanging rack or packed away in a suitcase and should never go home with the actors. You can assign one person to be responsible for cleaning any clothes that will be worn for more than one scene. All it takes is one actor to forget an essential piece of their wardrobe and filming is off the tracks before it even started for that day.

Regardless of which external audio device you use for recording dialogue, you will need to listen to and rename all the individual files. Even on a simple shoot this can get out of hand quickly. I suggest listening to the audio files each day and renaming them to match the scene and take of the shot. I would suggest keeping a notebook with the original file names and the corresponding scene/take name. This can be used as reference if you ever needed it.

You should also back up your audio files to an external hard drive and burn CDs of all the files each day.

Continuity can be wrecked by all kinds of small props and actions that may seem minor when filming but will come back to haunt you later. Cigarettes, candles, food, drinks, glasses and hand placements all have the potential for creating distracting errors. When it comes down to it, most people don't notice these things but I approach the subject with the desire to get things right. As soon as you start taking shortcuts and ignoring prop placements then that attitude can spread to larger areas. And as the old saying goes, "How you do anything, is how you do everything."

The position in the master shot of an actor resting their head in their hands can cause major problems if they don't repeat the gesture the same way and at the same moment in the subsequent close-up shots. Acting on film differs from stage work in this aspect tremendously. When an actor is on stage they get dozens of times to perform a certain role with dozens of small variations. The continuity on stage is character based, in film it is character *and* photography based. That is completely different. A film actor must craft a performance through focused control of their movements and words. Filming rehearsals will allow your actors to adjust to this and understand the importance of a controlled performance.

9

There is nothing more important than the safety of the cast and crew. This is the golden rule of filmmaking. At no point should the urgency of getting a shot ever put anyone in danger.

Safety is not just an on-the-set issue. One of the hardest parts of the filmmaking process is scheduling and you have to figure in the trip home for the cast and crew as well. It might be all right for an actor to take public transportation to the set during the day but then going home late at night isn't an option. Always have these issues settled before hand in case you need to supply a ride yourself or money for a cab. Safety is always number one.

10

If you are going to be filming in an apartment or in a way that will attract attention, talk to the neighbors beforehand. This is especially vital if you are working in an apartment since the potential for noise complaints is much greater. Letting them know what you are doing a few days earlier can help avoid confrontations and the loss of a shooting location.

Treat every location with respect and care. When you leave a location it should look better than when you arrived. There shouldn't be a single piece of trash left behind or any way to tell that you were there.

If you are using someone's house you can avoid tracking dirt into the house or damaging their floor by using slipcovers for your shoes. Painters use them and so do real estate agents. You just slip them over your shoes and you can walk in through the location without messing it up. They also work well for using when you are filming people walking and talking on a noisy surface. The actors can wear them and dampen the sound when their feet are not visible in the shot. You can buy a package of them at any hardware store and are just another tool to have at your disposal in order to maintain a clean set.

If you tell the owner of a location that you will be there from five until ten at night then stick to your word. You can find location agreement contracts online and you should use them. As with any contract work, consult a lawyer with any questions or concerns.

It is very important to stick to your word and get the work done. The time restrictions can help to energize your cast and crew to be as efficient, prepared and focused as possible.

Remember, lights used for filming get very hot. If you need to be out of a location by 10 o'clock you need to be shutting down the set with enough time to let the lights cool down, gear to be packed away and for actors to change out of their wardrobe. Time never moves quicker than it does on a film set so keep this in mind when scheduling location times.

13

Always have as a minimum: water and an accessible bathroom for your cast and crew. When filming inside it will get hot and the air will just hang there. You can get those small handheld fans for people to use in between takes or during breaks. The camera never lies; so if your cast is tired, overheated and their energy drained you better believe that the camera will pick this up. Even the smallest blink can seem enormous when captured by the camera. They may be saying all their lines correctly but if they are fading you have to do something. Keeping them hydrated and cool will go a long way to keeping the filming moving forward.

If there are changes to the filming schedule, send out an email AND call people to verify. Never assume people know something unless you can confirm it in person. The email will allow them to print the new information and the phone call can, hopefully, ensure that you know they have the information.

Voicemail messages don't count as the phone call. Only consider a direct conversation as a phone call.

Write out the exact message you need to give to people with the names of everyone in the cast and crew that needs a call. This way you can make sure everyone gets the same information *and* you can check off the names as you go.

15

As you start each day's filming you should take out your scene breakdowns and re-read the purpose statement for the scene. This can refresh your memory with what you need from the scene.

A couple of times we were running very low on time and had, as always, more to get done. I took out the scene breakdown and went through them. I had highlighted the few moments, lines of dialogue and basic information that were essential to the scene. A few times we were able to trim a scene down and get to the essence quickly without negatively affecting the storyline. I never would have been able to do this if I just had the full script sitting in front of me without being broken into smaller pieces. All I had to do was get those pieces done and we were covered.

16

It is invaluable to a film for you to slow down your mind and allow it to focus on the little things. Films are really just a collection of tiny moments. The film is connected by dialogue and by characters that are experiencing these tiny moments. If you ignore the little moments then your film simply won't work. Humor especially exists in these little moments. There is so much chaos and adrenaline on a set, even a small set with only a few people, that you can get focused on just getting shots done without attention to how they are getting done. You are always battling the loss of time, light, location access and the physical endurance of your cast and crew. All it takes is a car alarm screaming out over and over, an airplane slowly rumbling overhead or the neighbor's dog barking incessantly to rob your mind of focus.

Positive energy can be mutated into hostile frustration very easily. Having the ability to remain calm in the storm will help you immensely. Several times during filming an actor gave a subtle performance that found a new piece of humor or emotion and it would have slipped by without notice if I didn't constantly work from a calm place of focus and awareness. Listening and watching your actors regardless of the pressure weighing on you will save your film.

I always film the on-set warm up rehearsals. You might find a piece while editing that will help you for a cutaway or a piece of dialogue you can borrow. If the run-through is very informal you can just run camera and tail slate it as a rehearsal. When you do a full camera rehearsal I suggest running sound and reminding people when the camera is running it is considered a full take. Sometimes when people hear it is a rehearsal take for locking down camera movement or focus marks, the set gets noisy or unfocused. Everything you film has a chance of making it into the final cut of the movie, so every shot, rehearsal or not, should be treated as if it is a real take.

If you know a photographer that can lend their time, take whatever you can get. One of my biggest regrets was simply not taking enough on-set photos. The cinematographer and I are both photographers so we started off strong but it went away quickly. You can only devote so much attention to non-filming issues and as time went on the urgency of getting basic shots gave way to ignoring the small things. I regret this quite a bit. Luckily, I did about eight hundred photos with the cast in costume and then in street clothes before we began filming. Two days of filming we also shot extensive set photos so I did have enough to work with on a very basic level but I would never repeat that again.

I would suggest getting still photos of every day, each character in each costume on every set. As long as the person taking the photos knows how to behave on a set and can remain unseen and unheard, I would suggest making an effort to have them around as often as possible.

These photos should also include posed in-character shots on the set. You do not want to begin the process of creating web content, designing posters or marketing the film and have a shortage of images to work with. This is one of the biggest aspects of our shoot that I would have done completely differently.

Getting enough coverage of each scene is one of the biggest actions you can take that will help your film immensely. Not getting enough cutaways during filming could easily be one of the top three mistakes people make while filming their first feature. You will deeply regret not taking a few minutes for shots of the environment of wherever you are filming. Without some sort of shots to cut to, you will have no way of creating any variation on the scene.

I approach cutaways from several angles. The first is character based. Make sure you get a variety of reaction shots from everyone involved in the scene. It may not make any sense at the moment why someone would be smiling in a scene but when editing you may wish to show that character as more receptive and with that cutaway you can simply cut to that person smiling as a reaction shot to whatever was said and you have now created a new way in which that character exists. Without a variety of reaction shots and shots of characters simply sitting or standing on the set you will be unable to flesh out a scene or create nuances to a character's attitude.

The second type of cutaway is based on the environment. Ask yourself: what makes this particular location unique at this time of day and this time of year? Is it close to evening in the summer when all types of bugs swirl around the late afternoon sunrays? Is it a cold winter Monday morning when people are making their way to work through the wind and snow? Find some simple environmental shots that can help place the context of the scene to a location.

The last type of cutaway is a close-up of any small action. Say you are filming in a restaurant, what are the actions of a restaurant that can allow me to expand the specific action of the characters or can give the scene some individuality? Obvious shots of menus being set down or water being poured should be filmed to give you options. If any small actions happen such as a character holding something, make sure to get some shots of this as well. Let the shots last at the minimum of thirty seconds each, as this will give you enough room to work with them.

20

Just as the video side of each scene needs cutaways for ambience, you will need to record ambience or 'room tone' for each location. This is a fairly basic practice and isn't a new idea but people forget this all the time and it can come back to haunt you if you need it. I have worked on sets as an actor with first time directors and it is always a surprise how people don't realize that scenes are built in the editing room. Sound on the set should be as clean and quiet as possible. One of the reasons sets get so hot is that air conditioning units have to be turned off. It might seem like something small but it has to be done.

We missed turning off the air conditioning on only one set-up of one scene and it led to that dialogue needing to be re-recorded. Overall we did a good job as a large number of our scenes are inside but that one mistake led to a lot of work down the road. At the end of filming each day, get a good ten to fifteen minutes of uninterrupted location sound. This will allow you to have an actual background onto which you can place re-recorded dialogue or smooth over transitions that are uneven.

There will be a temptation to rewind and watch footage while you are filming but have not completely filled a MiniDV tape. If you are filming onto a hard drive or solid state this is not a problem but with tapes it can be disastrous. Say you filmed three takes of a scene and you go back to watch them, it can be very easy to not realize you are watching take two not take three and then stop watching your work, hit stop and now the tape is going to record over take three.

Another problem is breaking time code. If you watch a take and then hit stop past the point of the end of recording you will have broken the time code for the tape. This will prevent you from doing batch uploading and can add a lot of time to your editing process. The time code will reset and not recognize the next take as being minute twenty-three of the tape but as minute one of another tape. This may not sound like a big deal but when you are in the middle of capturing fifteen tapes of footage you will deeply regret breaking time codes.

Being efficient when filming will help you keep on schedule and focused. Videotape is not expensive but when it comes to staying focused you should act like it's the same price as gold. The digital age has created a mindset of not paying attention while taking pictures or filming video. It is just assumed you can take more pictures and there is no problem. I have been doing photography for a very long time. In fact, I had the same 35MM SLR camera for twenty-five years. I switched to digital in 2006 and I noticed the creative quality of my photos went down. I was used to having just twenty-four or thirty-six shots on a roll of film. It was costly and time consuming to buy the film, develop it and to make enlargements. My focus and attention were finely tuned to every shot when using film. Suddenly with a digital camera, I was shooting hundreds of pictures at one time and deleting as I went. However, my overall work was not as good. My focus went out the window when I knew I could just shoot more and more. It is important to get coverage and to film as much as you can but be conscious that just because you can film as much as you want doesn't mean what you are filming is good. Stay focused.

It is very important to stick to the script. Wandering off the map can be a disaster for many reasons. The most basic problem you will encounter will be trying to make sense of the dialogue while editing the film. If you allow each take to wander away from the script you will not be able to find any continuity within any scene. If the actors are not saying the same thing each take, then there may not be a logical place to cut to between takes or angles. Another problem comes in the possible loss of important plot points or basic information. There is a reason why you spend months or longer working on the script and then spend more time rehearsing. It isn't so you can get to the set and throw it all away.

I was able to smooth out some sound issues by either using a different audio take or by carrying over a line from a two-shot to a close up. These worked seamlessly because of consistent performances from the actors and from sticking to the script.

24

High quality video-assist can be an expensive item and could be beyond the budget of some productions. We were lucky enough to have a couple great monitors to work with and it helped immensely. The small viewing area on most video cameras does not accurately give you the entire filming frame. Making accurate movements and focus points is essential, so the larger the screen you have the better off you will be.

25

Whenever filming productions set up, the use of electrical power comes into play. My simplest piece of advice is: do not play with electricity. You can get careless or mess with it but I guarantee if you make a mistake, electricity will always win. It is fairly commonplace in smaller budget films to blow a fuse while working in a house or apartment. You should pay close attention to how many outlets you are using and where the extension cords are plugged in. More important than avoiding a blown fuse is avoiding someone getting seriously hurt or worse. Simply put: don't do things you are not qualified to do.

Cables running through a set are prime candidates for causing accidents. They are easy to trip on, possibly damaging equipment and much more importantly: hurting someone in the cast or crew. The first step is to make the cables secure. You can do this with either taping the cables down or using a cable runner. Tape works well but if you are worried about possible damage to a location floor then using the cable/cord runner works well. You can buy them at any office supply store and are usually used for keeping computer cables organized but they work well for this as well.

The next thing you should do is alert people working on the set of any possible hazards. Walk people through the set if there are multiple areas of concern. Remember cast and crew safety is number one so this is not an area you should ever cut corners on.

When you are out filming it is important to be prepared for last minute additions. Always carry a stack of extra/background actor release forms with you. If you find the need to add some depth to a scene or if people don't show up, you need to be prepared. Everyone you film needs to sign a release.

28

I always try to take actors aside when discussing a scene while filming. If you give directions in front of the rest of the cast and crew, it might make the actor feel as if they are being singled out. If I need to address an issue with an actor after a shot, I will make sure to give a quick note to the other actors to keep it balanced.

29

It is important to have actors run the scene from start to finish from several angles. I have worked as an actor on student films where they have chosen only certain dialogue sections to get in close up but you need to get as much coverage as you can get.

It is also important that the actors follow through the scene *in character* until you say, "cut." You won't know exactly where your edit points will be, so scenes should be played as far as possible to give you options.

As production ends, review your footage as soon as possible in order to let the actors know whether their work is done or not. You can count on needing them for audio work later on in the post-production phase but their appearance won't matter for that. There will be the possibility that the actors in your film will move on to other parts that might require them to change their appearance. It is in your best interest to review the footage as you go along and complete this process as soon after filming finishes as possible. The longer you wait the less likely the actors, crew, wardrobe, locations, etc. will be available and in continuity with your film.

POST-PRODUCTION

1

When you are working with digital media you must realize that it is a fragile medium. Saving and backing up your work needs to happen every minute and day, respectively. You can never save your work enough and you can never finish an editing session without backing up what you did. Make it part of your routine and never get lazy with it. Never. This is one reason I prefer to use cameras that have MiniDV tapes. No matter what happens to the files I always have the tapes. I can always go back to the source and start again. Don't assume a disaster won't happen to you. People have given you the most precious thing that exists on Earth: their time. Respect them by protecting everyone's work every day.

2

Patience and dedication are needed to make it through the editing process. When working with digital editing, especially high definition (HD), rendering times add up. It isn't healthy to sit in a chair for hours without getting up. Not to mention your eyes will get wonky very quickly.

Because I was editing full-time I was spending a lot of time working in a computer chair. I began having trouble seeing and focusing on distant objects. Not good. Because I also have back issues I got into a routine of getting up and stretching every fifteen minutes. Every few hours I would take a thirty-minute break. I also did this when rendering large files as they can take an hour to complete sometimes. I'd walk up and down the stairs, stretch out on the floor, take my dog for a walk, do some push-ups, whatever it took to get out of the chair and get the blood flowing again.

3

In pre-production you should have made notes about a trailer, such as the images or lines you thought would be good to use. Take your notes and put together a simple trailer. Find the essence of your story and see how it plays. What tone are you going for? If you can capture the essential moments and the tone in a trailer at the beginning of editing, you can go back and watch it as you go to remind yourself what you are building.

Making a trailer for the world to see should be a highly focused effort. Without a recognizable name you will be judged solely on content. A bad trailer will leave you dead in the water. If you have made a horror film the trailer should convince people that they are not going to sleep for days after watching your film. If it is a comedy it should highlight non-story element humor so people laugh but you don't ruin big moments for characters. Making people laugh or scaring the hell out them will bring attention to your film no matter how small the budget was.

4

First impressions could make or break your film. Without stars or big-budget effects, the interest your film will generate will come from how unique and well produced it looks. You will not be able to take back what damage you do if you put out a trailer before you have figured your film out yet. Bad technical work or an unfocused story can kill your movie before you are even done editing it.

5

One area of the film that you can't get around is spending money on software during editing. A couple programs I used literally saved my film and I highly recommend them. We were able to get mostly clean video but the nature of video will include visual noise. We shot a lot of outside scenes at night, which were a challenge to say the least. The video cleaning program Neatvideo absolutely is essential in my opinion. At the time of this book's release, this plug-in program is $100. It is worth ten times that and maybe more. It is simple to use but it will allow you to save footage that you would swear won't work because of bad picture quality.

6

Another plug-in that can be overused very easily but at the same time can be an amazing tool is "Looks" by MagicBullet. Color correcting has take on a life of its own because of video. The moving image is now seen as still images are for graphic designers. You can manipulate the video in a million ways but this can also lead to over-processed video. The Looks plug-in is expensive so it is not for everyone but it is a powerful and amazing tool that will allow you to create the exact color nuances and style you want.

As far as audio goes, an essential program I used was made by Bias and is called SoundSoap. There is a standard version and a more expensive Pro version; either are worth buying. I have both and use them for almost every audio project I work on. I can easily say that this program saved our film by removing background noises and distracting ambient sound. We somehow managed to have recorded great audio on set but it still needed improvement.

One of my biggest regrets during filming was not having an experienced person doing sound throughout the film. We managed to do a good job overall but you can only take luck so far. Having an experienced sound/boom operator is essential and I will never do sound by committee again. We managed to get good sound because Jason (the D.P.), Tony and I had some experience and we had great equipment. Also, the people who helped caught on quickly and were very serious about doing a good job. If we hadn't been so lucky the entire sound for the film could have been unusable. The moral of the story is: do not film without an experience sound person.

8

The important thing to remember with these great editing programs is that they are there to put the finishing touches on good video and audio. If you don't have usable files to begin with than nothing will help you. Never assume that software is going to save the day and it's acceptable to be lazy when filming. If you don't capture good video and audio in the first place, no program is going to save you.

9

At some point people are going to want to see what you have been editing. Until a good deal of it is done I would not show any footage to people. The average person has absolutely no idea how much work goes into making a movie and how much of it is actually done after the filming is complete. People who work in post-production are true artists and craftsman and you will come to appreciate their abilities very quickly. Your hard work may be sabotaged by showing people unfinished parts of the film without context, then becoming upset that they didn't respond well to what they saw. Every editing room is different so the number of people will vary but I would be very careful about sharing footage early on in the editing process.

10

Not everyone works in a linear way but I prefer to work straight through the film myself. Because I have worked in short films for so long I am used to being able to tackle the film from start to finish fairly easily. Features are a whole different game and it is up to you how you want to approach your workflow. You may need to start with a certain scene or actor's part since you will be losing them and any re-shoots will need to be determined quickly. I suggest just working from start to finish and this will allow you to at least share the opening sequence with people in the cast and crew to let them know you have successfully moved onto the editing process. It is important to let the cast and crew know how your progress is going so they can still feel connected to the film.

I would suggest that no one outside the cast and crew, except maybe a trusted family member, see the unfinished footage. At some point you will need to show people if you are unsure of a scene or need a second opinion. I would find one person you trust who is knowledgeable and stick with them. This will allow you to have a consistent voice to receive feedback from and doesn't need to be brought up to speed with each new scene as to what they are seeing.

12

Always go the extra mile for the film. When you encounter a problem you will have to make a decision and I suggest you always do what it takes to make the film the best it can be. Some people shy away from asking actors to do re-shoots or reworking a scene from scratch. If the potential exists to correct or improve something, you should always do it.

This approach saved our film completely. I went back and filmed a few transitions, augmented a scene, rewrote and re-filmed an entire scene and then re-recorded the complete dialogue for four and a half scenes. This was spread out over quite a few months also but it had to be done. I got the film to a rough cut and realized certain audio issues existed. I could have left them but that is not how I work.

The landlord scene was originally filmed in a very silly way that worked with other quick little scenes involving the two main characters basically screwing around avoiding work. We had a bunch of small bits planned but only filmed a few because of time running out. Then when placed in context of the film, the tone of those silly scenes was completely out of place.

I made the decision to re-film the scene but we no longer had access to the apartment we used for the film originally. Another problem existed in the fact that Austin, the actor who played Eddie, had a small mohawk haircut for a play he was in at the time. Tony, the actor who played Max, has a couch that looks similar to the one in the apartment we shot in and we decided to make that work somehow. In the original apartment we used a school desk that was a center of focus. It was Tony's old school desk, so we dug it out of the garage again and placed it in Tony's apartment. His floors were similar to the original apartment, so it was close enough.

Since the scene takes place in the late afternoon and the following scenes clearly show the sun brightly shining before setting I knew I could adjust the color somewhat. Austin's character wears a hat in the second half of the film once they leave their apartment, so it hadn't been introduced yet. To cover Austin's mohawk, I had him put the hat on and ask Max (Tony) if he liked his new purchase. The previous scene had them arguing about their lack of money for rent, so it allowed for narrative continuity and some humor while at the same time covering Austin's hair.

I kept the basic dialogue of the scene for Max and Eddie but since we only had the ability to shoot their angle of the film I had to reuse the footage of the landlord entering and speaking. I made a scratch version of the scene and played it on a laptop at the correct eye-line and level for Austin and Max. I simply played the video and had them act opposite the original footage.

I then took the footage and applied a nice golden glow from the sun that would be streaming through the window. I took the original audio and close-ups of the landlord and cut it in. The scene plays much better within the tone of the film and matches easily enough to work.

The lesson to learn from that experience is: when you make a scene that is very specific tonally, you need to make sure that you are set on it. Without having variations you are locked into that original tone. The other thing to realize is that the average person does not watch a film the same way a filmmaker does. The saving grace of those re-shoots was that the scene is very energetic and contains a lot of information being given. The two main characters are being evicted from their apartment and your focus stays with them. What this means is that people won't notice the lack of production or minor errors if they care about what they are watching.

A movie like "Clerks" (1993, Kevin Smith) is a perfect example of this. People get so locked into the character's individuality and expressiveness. No one even notices the first time watching the film that several people play multiple roles. I'm not saying you can make mistakes by having lots of jokes or distractions but don't let a small issue stop you from moving forward. Get creative and find a solution to your problem.

14

Conversely, if you are relying on something small or something in the background to have a big effect on the film then you are going to be in trouble. If something is important within the narrative, it needs to be treated that way.

Re-recording dialogue, also known as ADR (additional dialogue recording) or looping, is incredibly difficult to do well. There is no way to sugar coat this aspect of editing. Knowing this should make you work even harder during filming to make sure you get quality sound to begin with. To make a feature film without doing any ADR is impossible or at least close to it. We came very close with some skill and a profound amount of luck. However, I made the decision to attempt to re-record not just a few lines here and there but four whole scenes.

This is a difficult process but it allows your actors to complete their performance with controlled nuances and clearly delivered lines. Both of these are essential elements of a successful film. Much like the re-filming of the landlord scene I exported the scenes and uploaded them to Vimeo.com. This allowed me to share the scenes with actors in a password protected way. I transcribed the scenes from the various takes I needed, emailed the actors the text along with the links to the videos. I made sure they got these well in advance of the recording sessions so they could practice. This helped us immensely as it is not something you can just show up for, attempt to wing it and hope to be successful.

For re-recording the dialogue, I built a vocal booth for $20. I took a three panel cardboard presentation board (the kind you use for school science fair projects), lined it with a foam pad, and cut a rectangle viewing area in it. I bought a plastic front from a picture frame and covered the hole.

In my office I have a closet with sliding doors, so I simply opened them half way, had the actor step in and placed the panel so it closed off the closet. I have two computer monitors so I placed one of them on a stand so the person in the "vocal booth" could look straight through the window and see the screen perfectly. We used a headphone hub that allowed both the actor and I to hear the scene as it played. We placed the microphone on a mic stand aimed into the booth at the same distance and angle as we did in filming so it could match the overall sound quality of the original shoot.

I simply played the clips through Final Cut Pro at the desk while they watch the monitor. It was hard work but we managed to have great audio in four scenes that otherwise would have brought the film down.

If you find that you are lacking a transition shot or need something to add to a specific location consider using stock footage. There are some great web sites that have large amounts of various footage you can purchase for use in your film.

I had shot some general establishing and transitional footage but needed some more. We shot our film in late summer and by the time I was completing the rough cut the seasons had changed. So going back out and filming more exterior shots was not possible. I found plenty of great footage on the stock site http://www.pond5.com. I am now loading up my own stock footage to their database as well.

18

One very important aspect of editing is the need to take time away from the film. At some point you will find yourself just re-watching scenes and not making much progress. It may not even seem to make sense after awhile. Don't be afraid, after putting in a lot of work editing, to walk away for a few days. Stepping away from the film for a few days after wrestling with it for weeks or months is a healthy part of making sense of what you have accomplished.

Take some notes before you step away with any issues you may have and make them as specific as possible. Take time to describe what you think is not working with the film and why. Also make a list of what the strengths are in the film and why you think they work. Then step away and spend a few days doing anything but thinking about the movie.

When you return to the film you will have, hopefully, a fresh mind to see and hear the film. Take out the notes you made before you stepped away and review them. Are those areas still problems to you? Your subconscious is always working on the problems of your life so, after some time away you may find the solution is sitting in your mind waiting for you.

20

When you have finished a rough cut it is time to show someone your hard work. I would suggest two small screenings: one for the cinematographer and some cast members and the second for a few close friends and family members. People involved in the project may end up just watching their work in the film as actors often do but their reactions are still worth noting. Your friends and family will have no connection to the filming process and will be seeing it in a completely different way.

21

The important thing to do before screening the film for people is to mention up front what areas still need work or any specific technical things they need to know so they don't get hung up on them while watching. For example if the title sequence isn't complete let them know. You don't want them negatively wondering, "Is that how it is going to look?" Preface the screening with all the information they need to make sense of what you are showing them. Secondly, when you get feedback from them make sure you have specific and detailed questions prepared to ask them. Often when people give feedback they will say "It was good" or "I liked it." Both of which are nice but not helpful at this stage of the editing process. Just as you made a list of problems and strengths before taking a break, this same list should be used as direct questions to the people at the viewing.

Most of the time you will not need to even ask when things are not working because you will know just from watching it. There is a palpable energy when a scene is too long, the narrative is confusing or the jokes don't work. Make sure you make your own notes about how you feel while watching the film with others. Your gut will tell you if something is just not right.

From your pre-production work and your scene breakdown packets, you should have purpose statements for each scene as well as the complete film itself. You can have them write out what they felt the purpose statements for each of the scenes were and compare that to what you were hoping to achieve. Take the time to listen to what they have to say, and then trust your gut with what actions you will take.

I was lucky to have worked in music for some time and have experience recording both music and audio. It takes time to understand how to properly mix and layer audio and there simply isn't enough space here to get into a detailed discussion of it. Your audio has to be taken seriously though and once again, if you don't have the answers or the skill find someone who does. Audio is easily the single biggest technical factor that will lose people's interest in your film. Just like the video this is a two-part process. The first part is what you record on the set and the second part is what you do with that audio in the editing room.

You will have to decide how to handle the music in your film. A common approach is to have some key songs from various bands combined with original music written specifically for the film. This is not always possible unless you are lucky enough to have a budget that allows for someone to score the film. Don't even think about using songs from well-known bands, as it will never happen without absurd amounts of money.

I am a proponent of variety and diversity. Just as it is important to explore personal ideas in your films within the unique world you live in, music is a great way to explore your local scene. If it is possible, explore the local music scene and see if any bands fit into your vision of the soundtrack.

When you have reviewed all the feedback from the screenings, made any changes it is time to take one final break from the film. I would not think about the film for a week. Absolutely nothing involving the film should enter your mind. After the week is over, sit down, fire up the computer and watch it straight through. What does your gut tell you? Being sick of it, unwilling to work harder by tackling another challenge, or being anxious about the world seeing it aren't reasons to take action. Only what your gut tells you can truly be the answer. If there is more work to do, then do it. If you feel in your gut that the film is done, then it is time for the world to finally see your hard work. Regardless of what the world thinks though this last viewing is for your self. It is time to take a moment and realize you have set goals and achieved them. No one can take away the fact that you have accomplished this. You have moved from the category of people who talk about making a movie to the category of people who have actually made a movie. Congratulations. Now the fun, frightening and truly hard part begins: getting people to see your movie.

WHEN THE FILM IS DONE

I suggest making postcards at any time during production. If you haven't made them yet, you should once the film is done. They are good to handout or leave in coffee shops, movie theaters or anywhere you can put them. You should never leave the house without a stack.

Only put web addresses, contact information or non-dated information, this way you won't be left with a ton of outdated postcards. Whenever anyone asks you about your movie you can hand them all the necessary information in a clear and professional way. I have used http://www.1000spostcardprinting.com several times and I have always been happy with their work. At the time of this writing, they have five-thousand color, double-sided postcards for $95.

2

At this point you should look back to your notes on who the target audience for your film was and then go find them. With a small Indie film, it is always best to start small and grow in steps. Hollywood uses the shotgun approach and aims their ads at every single person on the planet. You have to be smarter and without the enormous advertising budget of a studio film, you have no choice but to focus in and use word of mouth.

A way to do this is to literally start with your immediate world and move outward. Don't be afraid to knock on your neighbor's door and let them know what you accomplished. If you are able to start on your street and keep moving up and up, you can feel that you are accomplishing something tangible. Placing expensive ads doesn't let you know that people are actually seeing or retaining the information. Meeting someone face to face in the beginning of promoting the film can help you build confidence and give you experience in speaking clearly and concisely about your movie.

3

This is the time to get out your list of goals for the film. Now the film is done you can assess whether the film you made still fits with where you wanted it to go. It is possible that you had planned to submit the film to every festival you could but after viewing the final edit it just doesn't feel right. Conversely, you may realize that you have captured lightning in a bottle and have surprised yourself with how good the film turned out. A screening for the cast and crew can help you decide if you are unsure. If the cast is excited and everyone is dedicated to getting the word out then you should accept the help and see how far you can take the film.

It is incredibly important to stick to the promises you made to the cast and crew. If you promised everyone a copy of the DVD by a certain time then stick to it. If you run into obstacles that force you to reschedule your timeline then make sure you communicate this to everyone. You cannot promote the film successfully by yourself, so if you lose the confidence of the cast and crew you are sunk. They will not take promoting the film seriously if they perceive that you are not taking them seriously. There has to be a sense of organized urgency when editing. Set realistic goals at the beginning of the project and stick to them.

5

Once the film is done and you have locked in a final edit, get a hold of your local paper. Let them know it is done, what screenings you have planned and invite them. You can also plan to show it to several press people in a separate screening just for them. You can invite some of the cast also and make them available afterwards for interviews and photos.

6

Take time to build a network of fellow artists. Contact the actor and crew database with news of your finished film and where they can see the trailer or attend a screening. Thank them again for showing interest in your film and ask them what they have done artistically since the auditions. Ask if they have any new work that can be seen online, take the time to watch it and share a positive comment afterwards.

7

Take the time to send out hand-written 'thank you' cards to everyone directly involved in making the film. Email is efficient and immediate but impersonal. It's a classy way to let someone know you appreciate their work. People will remember receiving something in the mail much more than an email.

If you have decided not to pursue film festivals and want to control the release of the film yourself, consider using Createspace.com. They are run by Amazon and create CDs, books, and DVDs on-demand and ship them for you. They also have an online movie rental service. I use them and could not have been happier with the results. The quality is first rate, you don't have to worry about inventory or shipping, you set the price and everyone knows and trusts shopping through Amazon.

9

Visit a local college and talk to the theater and film departments. If the film turned out successfully you can offer your services as a real world example of creating a film. At the very least they might be able to hang up a poster for a screening you are having.

10

You will never be able to successfully market the film and spread the word by yourself. If you handled the filming process professionally and treated everyone with respect and kept to your promises, you should be able to rally the cast and crew together to promote the film. The single best way to get anything out into the world is through word of mouth. Emphasize how important it is for everyone involved to reach out to their immediate world and let them know about the film. Often with smaller Indie movies, after the filming is complete the cast and crew never see each other again. Hopefully the filming process was a positive one and it bonded all of you together. If this was the case then carry that camaraderie into marketing the film.

It may be difficult to think of what your next project will be so soon after finishing the one you are trying to get people to see. However, it is an important part of building momentum for future work. If you are planning a career in filmmaking then part of promoting this film will be about your future plans. You will be invariably asked, "What's next?" If you are lucky then you have a script ready to go but most likely you will just have a general idea. That's fine and that's all most people want to hear. Simply saying "I'm making a horror film" will be good enough. This lets you plant the seeds for your next film; something you couldn't do with your first one.

12

Sit down with the director of photography and watch the film. Discuss what worked, what didn't and why. Make specific notes about the positives and negatives and then consult your production journal as to that days shooting to see what may have affected it.

Ask your cast their opinions about how the entire process went from the auditions to the screening. Compile all these notes and review them before your next film. Each project you work on is a learning experience whether it is your first film or your tenth. Let these notes help guide you to a successful next project.

If you meet someone about to start their first film, take time to sit down with them and share your experiences. All good things in life come from helping other people. A great way to build working relationships is to reach out and help others. The notes you made about the good and the bad are a great place to start. This can give you some specifics to share and will be a good springboard for more involved discussions.

14

Take time to organize everything you learned from this experience. The process of writing your thoughts down will help you articulate to others what it is you achieved and what you expect from your next project. If you feel that your experiences may be valuable to others then create a book like I did. Take your journey to another level by finding ways to connect and help others.

15

Sit back and enjoy doing nothing for at least a day or two. The first day you don't have a 'to-do list' will be a very rewarding day. No one can take away what you have accomplished.

Take some time to enjoy your work, catch up on your sleep and then after a day or so when you find yourself going out of your mind from boredom, go back to page one of this book, add your personal notes to mine and start all over again!

POSTERS AND MARKETING

For full color versions of these posters please visit:
anymomentproductions.com

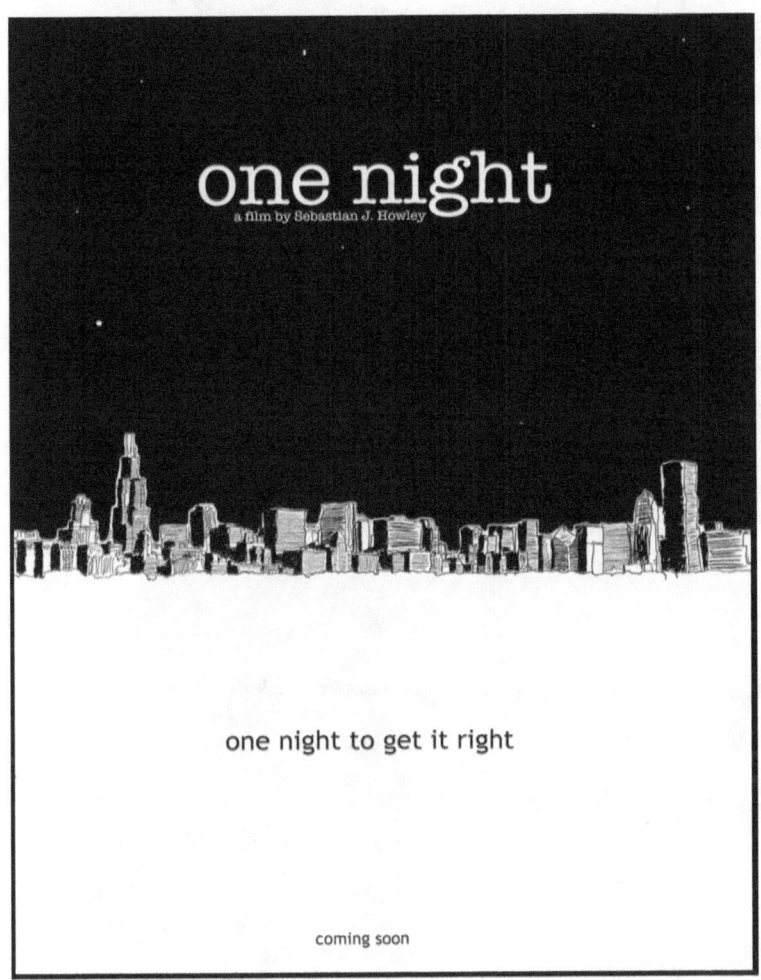

Original poster concept

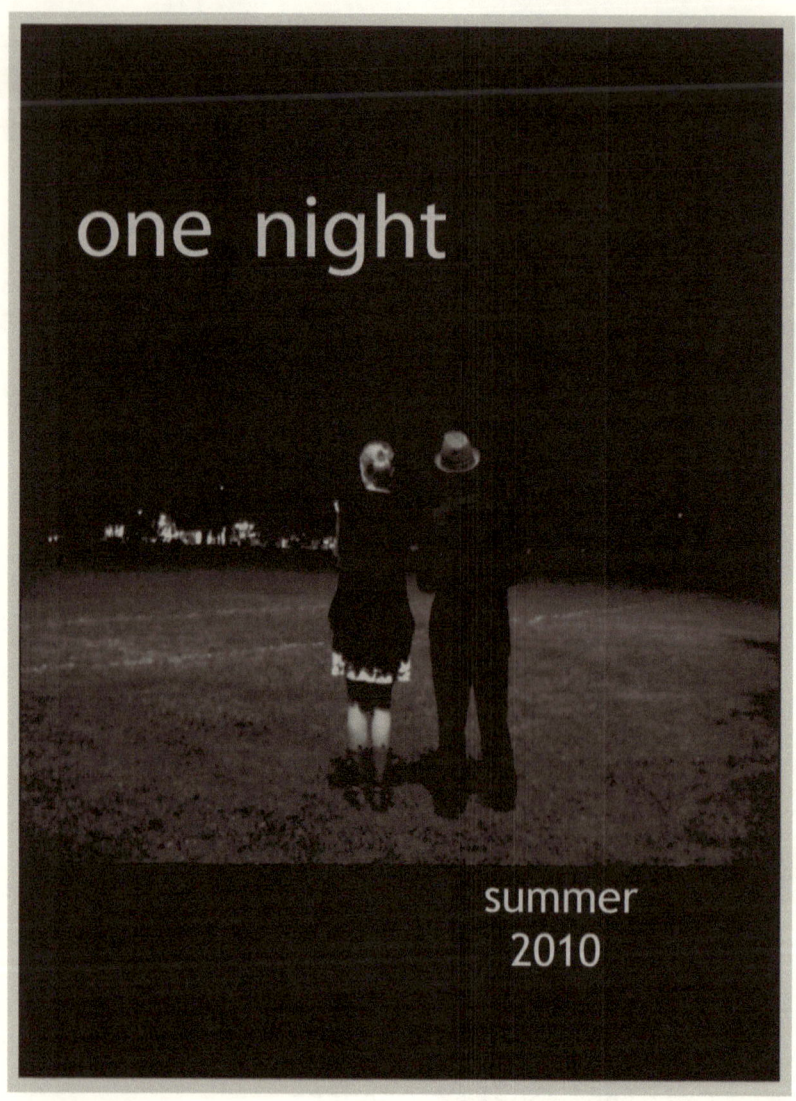

Preview poster with screenshot

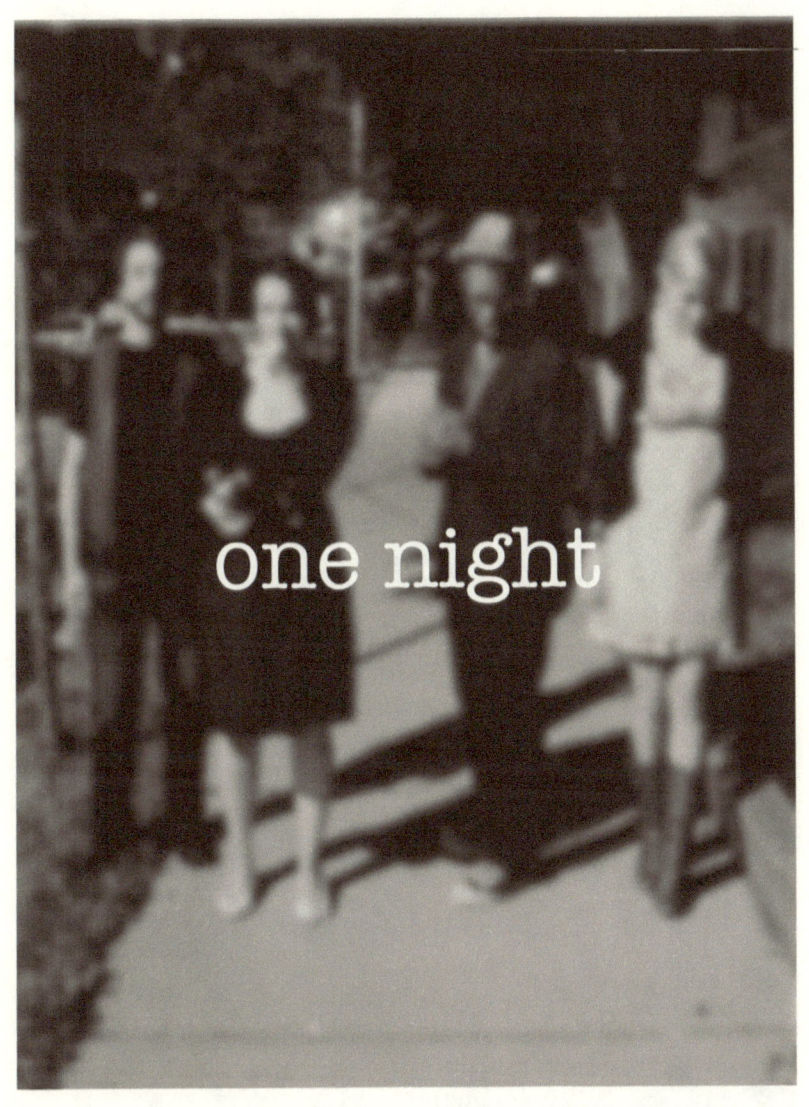

one night

First official poster released

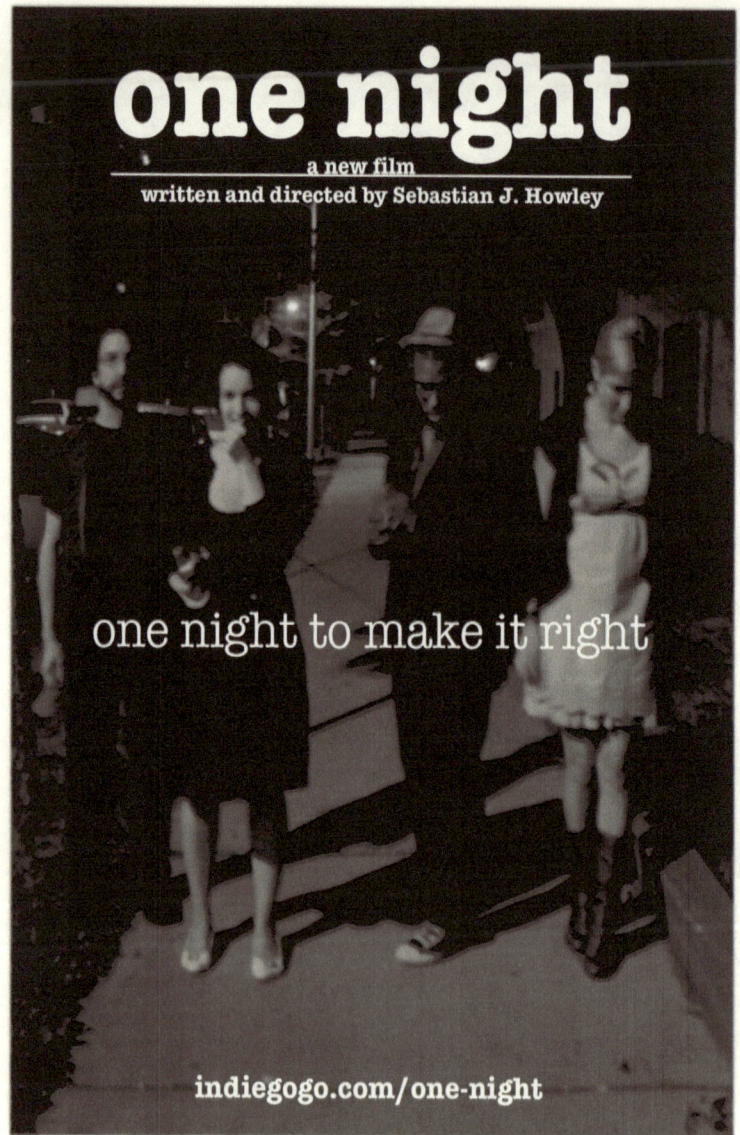

Promo Postcard

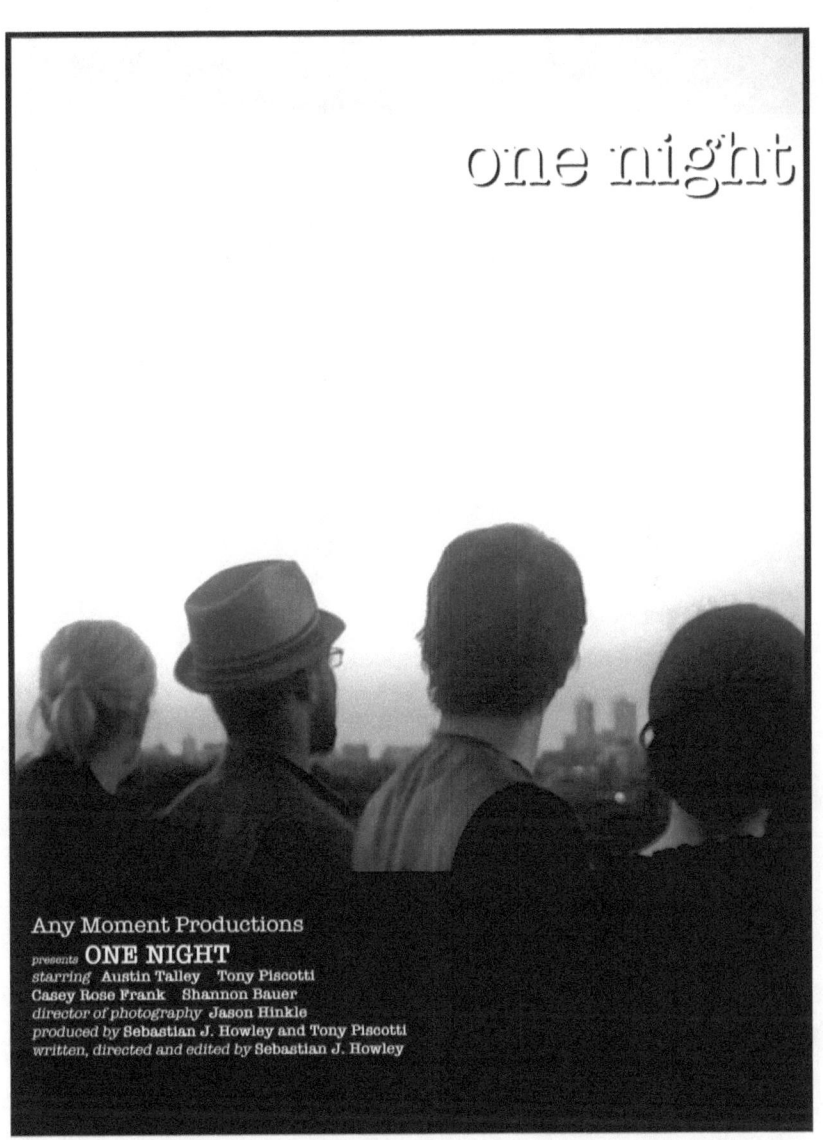

one night

Any Moment Productions
presents **ONE NIGHT**
starring **Austin Talley   Tony Piscotti**
Casey Rose Frank   Shannon Bauer
director of photography **Jason Hinkle**
produced by **Sebastian J. Howley and Tony Piscotti**
written, directed and edited by **Sebastian J. Howley**

Official final poster

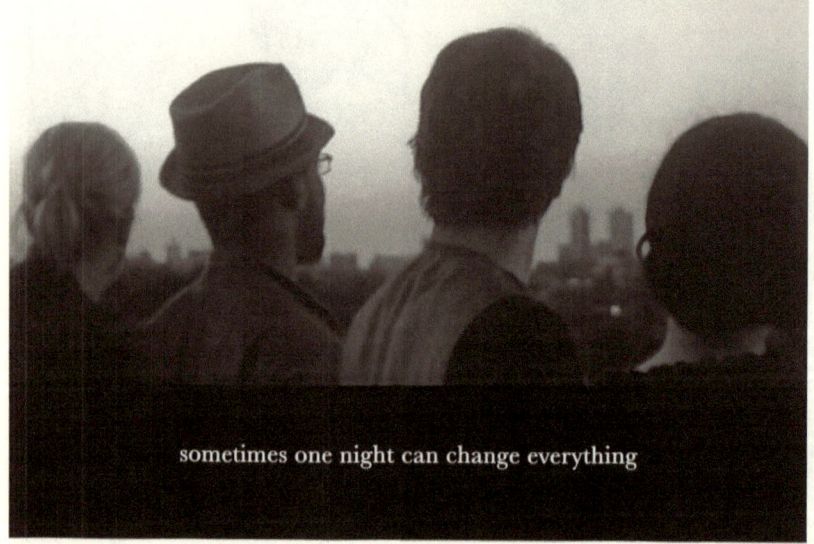

Any Moment Productions *presents*

one night

sometimes one night can change everything

DVD cover with new tag line:
"sometimes one night can change everything"

CAST PHOTOS

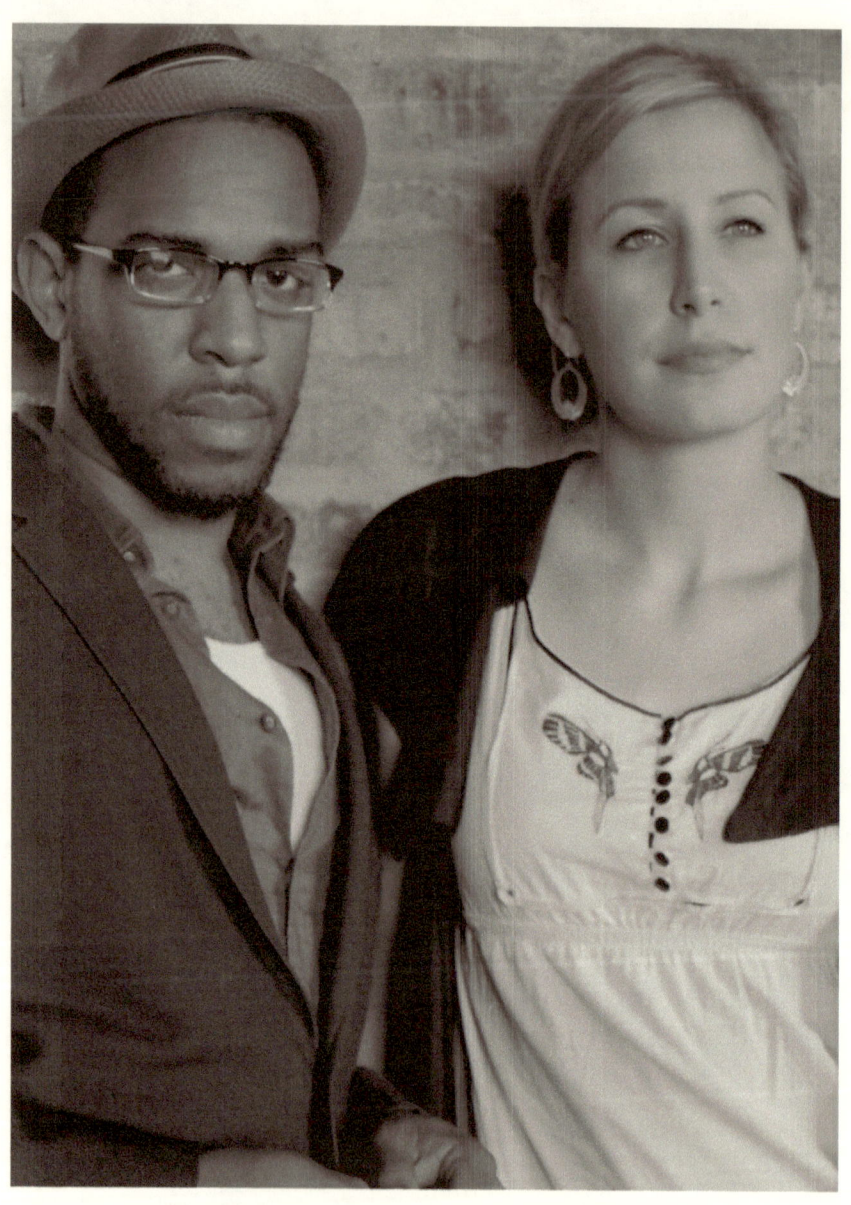

Austin Talley and Shannon Bauer

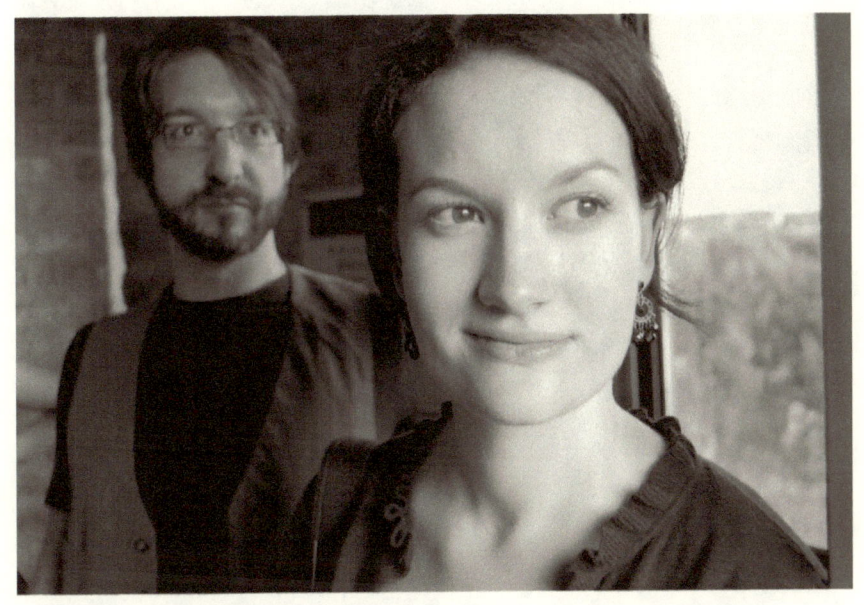

Tony Piscotti and Casey Rose Frank

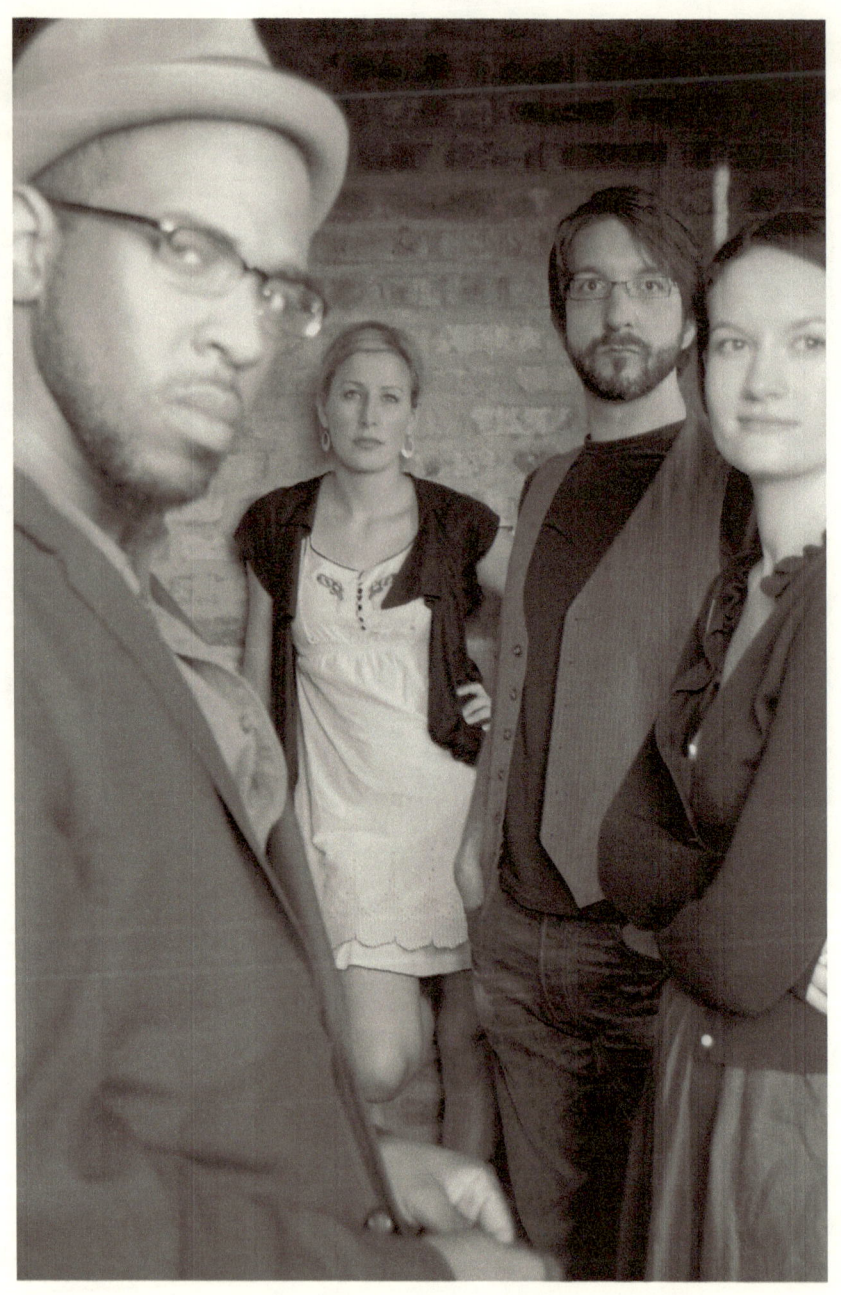

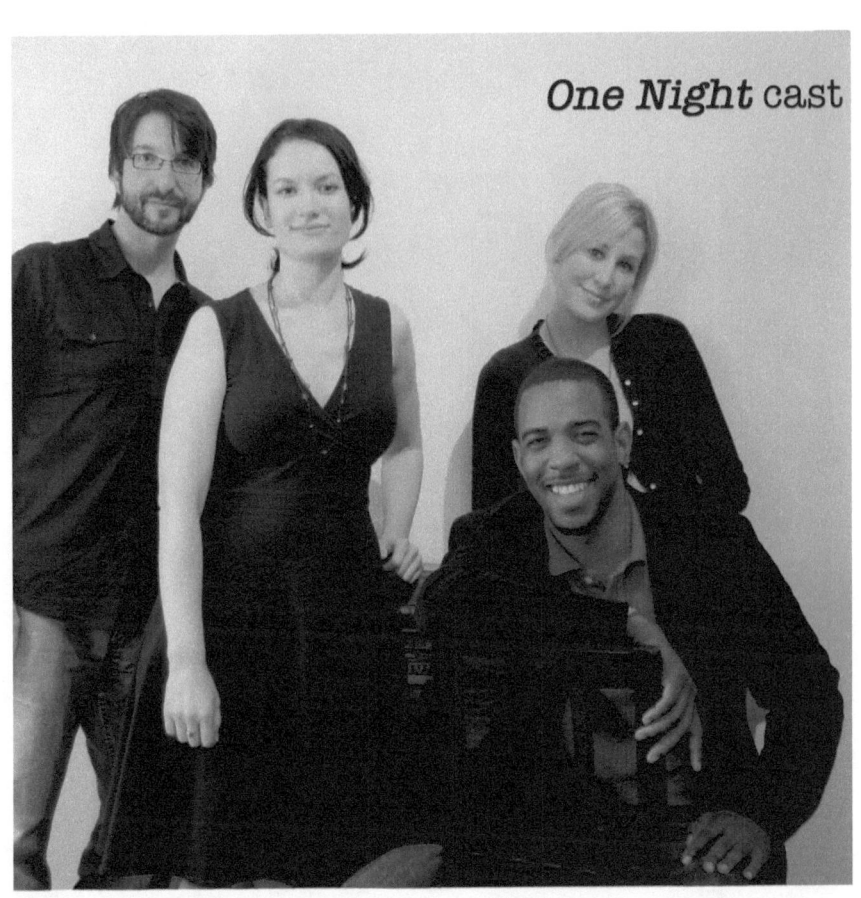

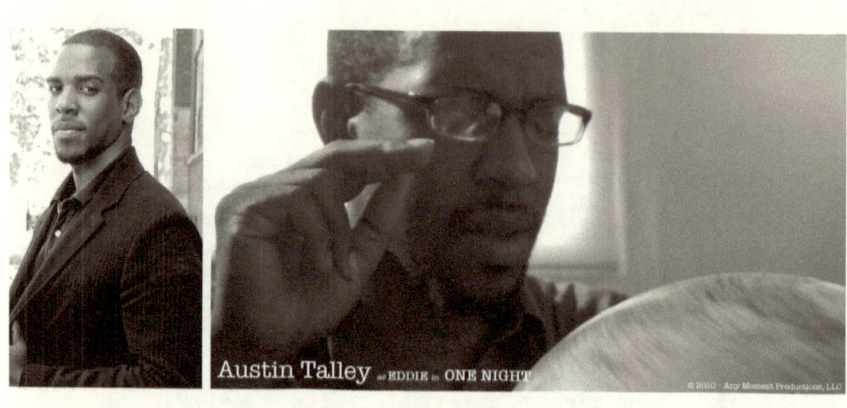

Austin Talley *as* EDDIE *in* ONE NIGHT

© 2010   Any Moment Productions, LLC

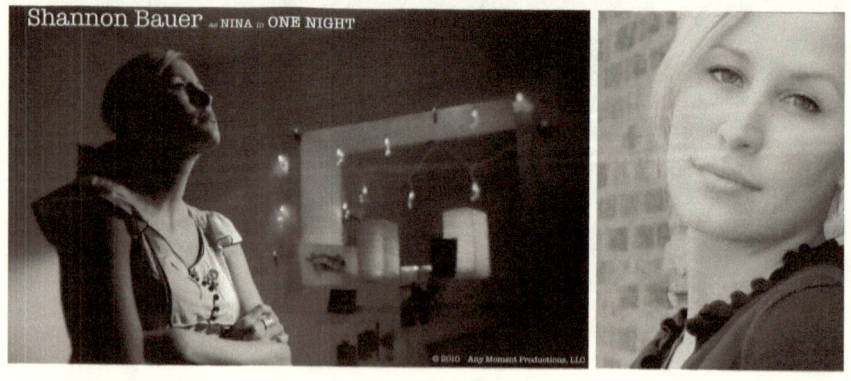

Shannon Bauer *as* NINA *in* ONE NIGHT

© 2010   Any Moment Productions, LLC

Character Profiles for Social Media Posting

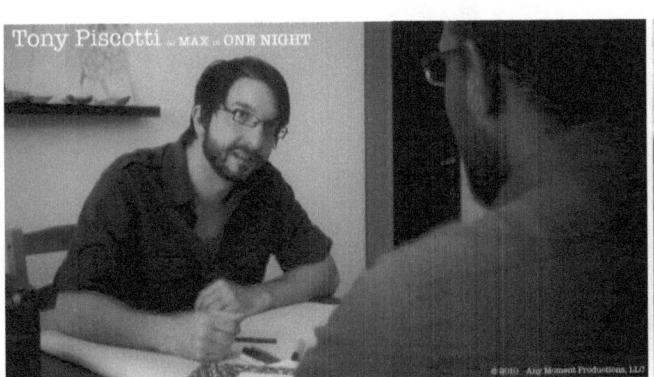

Tony Piscotti as MAX in ONE NIGHT

© 2010 Any Moment Productions, LLC

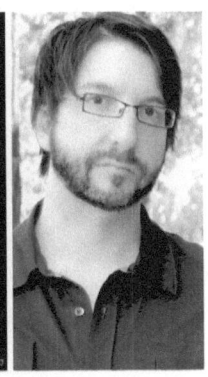

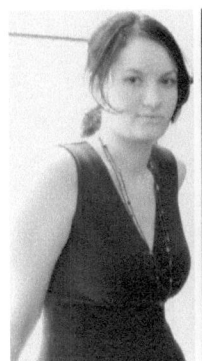

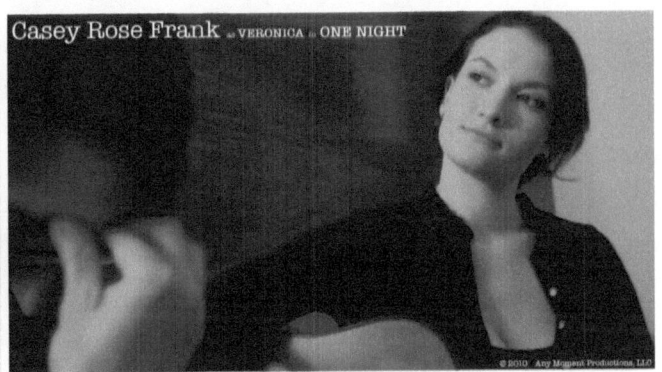

Casey Rose Frank as VERONICA in ONE NIGHT

© 2010 Any Moment Productions, LLC

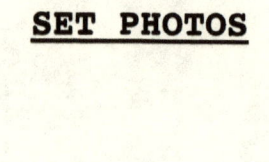

SET PHOTOS

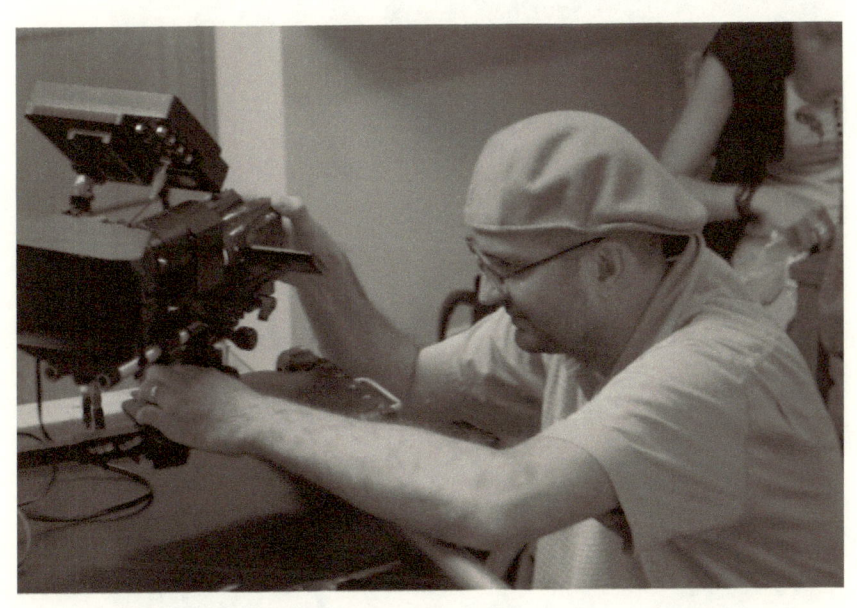

D.P. Jason Hinkle sets up the camera

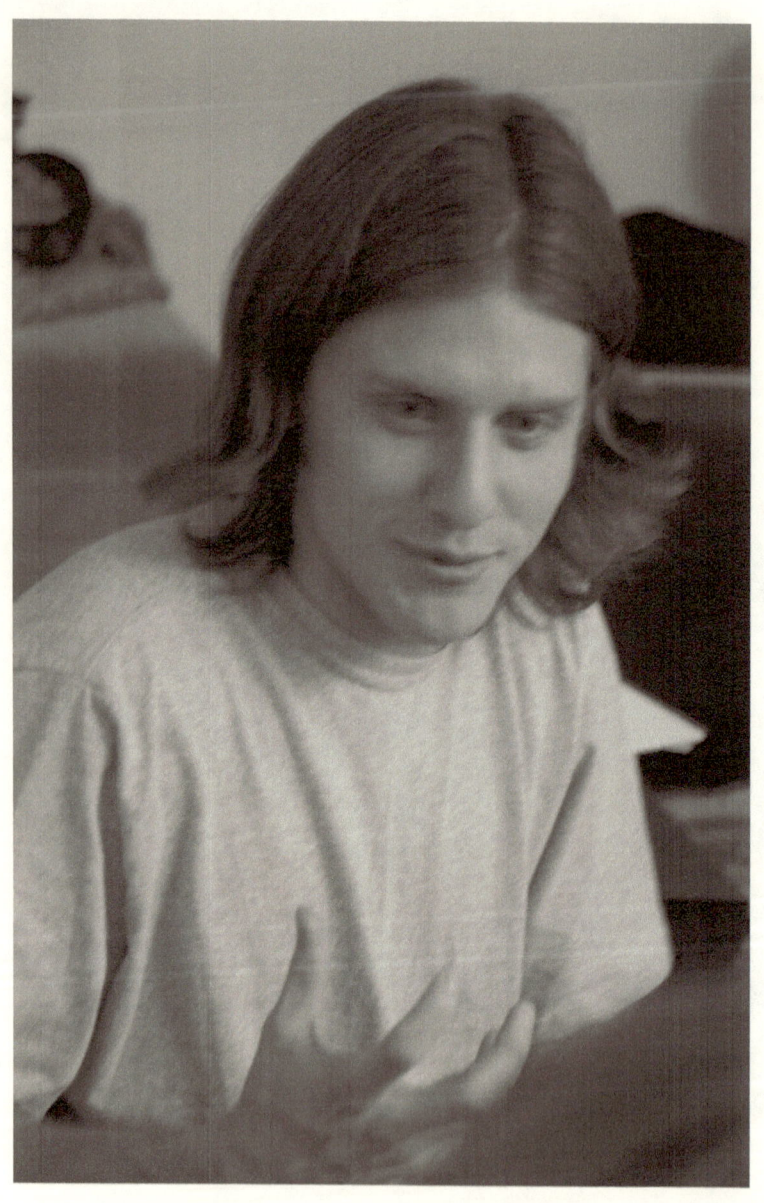

Actor George Christopher discusses a scene

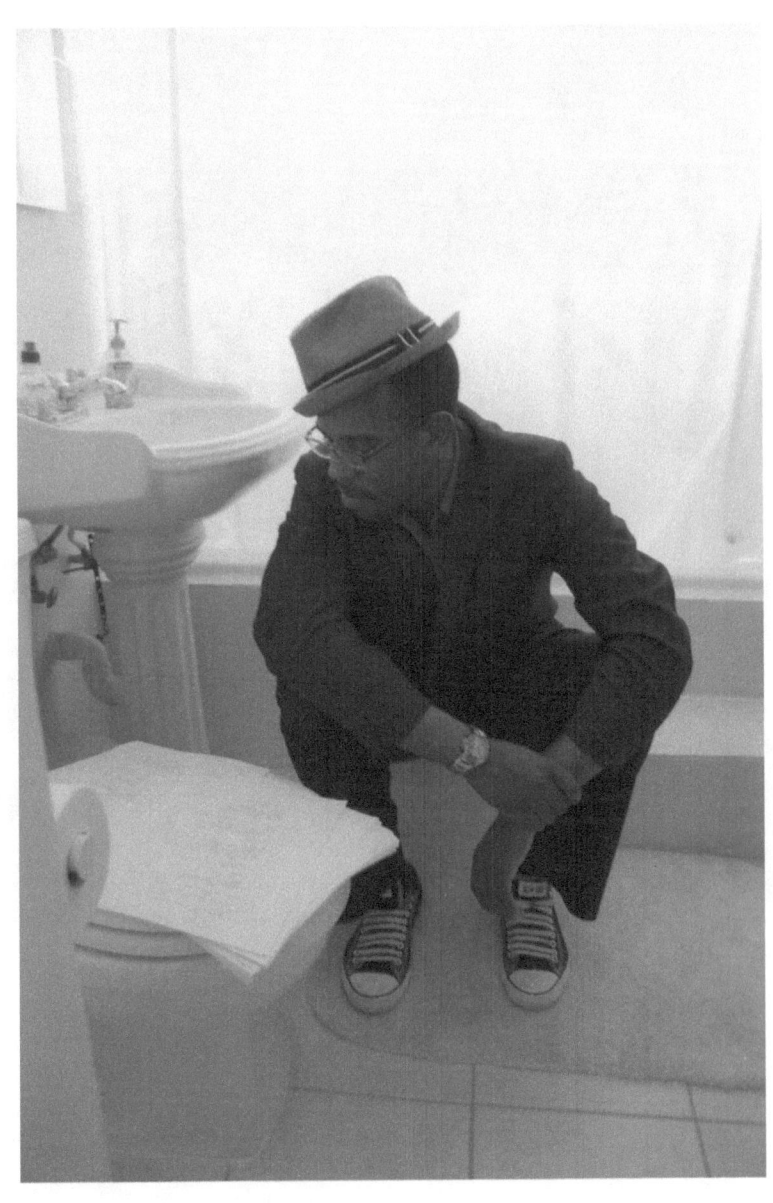

Austin Talley does last minute script work

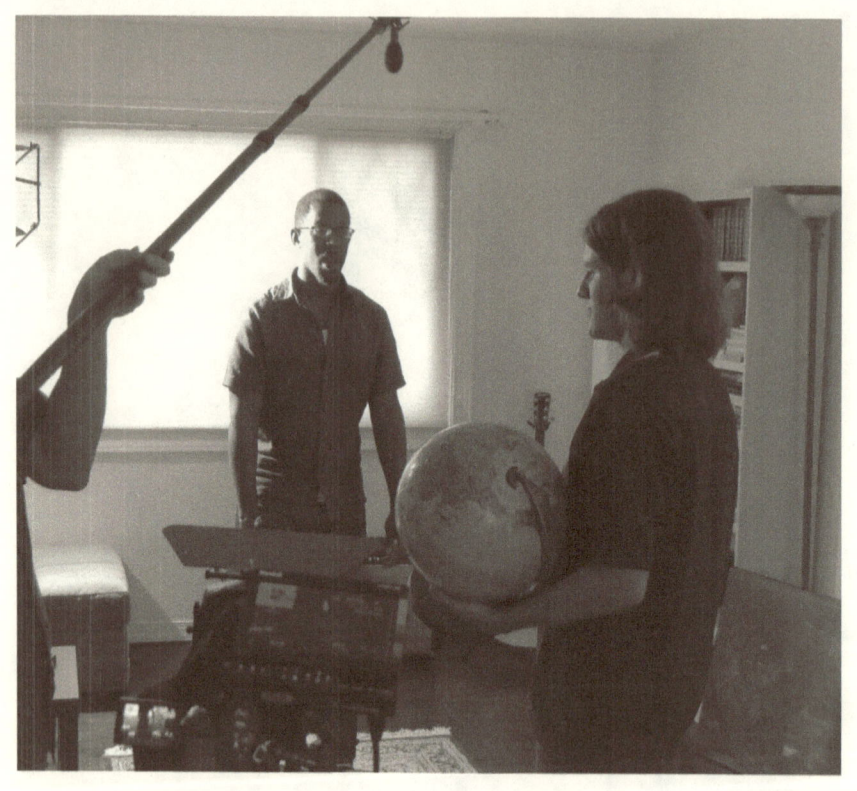

On the set for the first day of filming

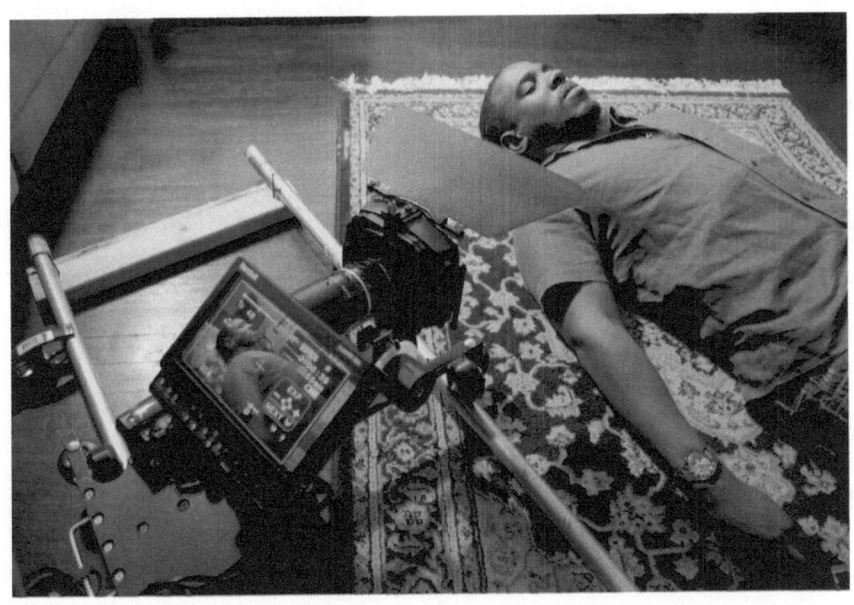

The simple homemade dolly rails made set-up
quick and easy, while allowing for quality
controlled camera movements. The video
assist on top of the camera was expensive
but an essential tool for composition, focus
and lighting.

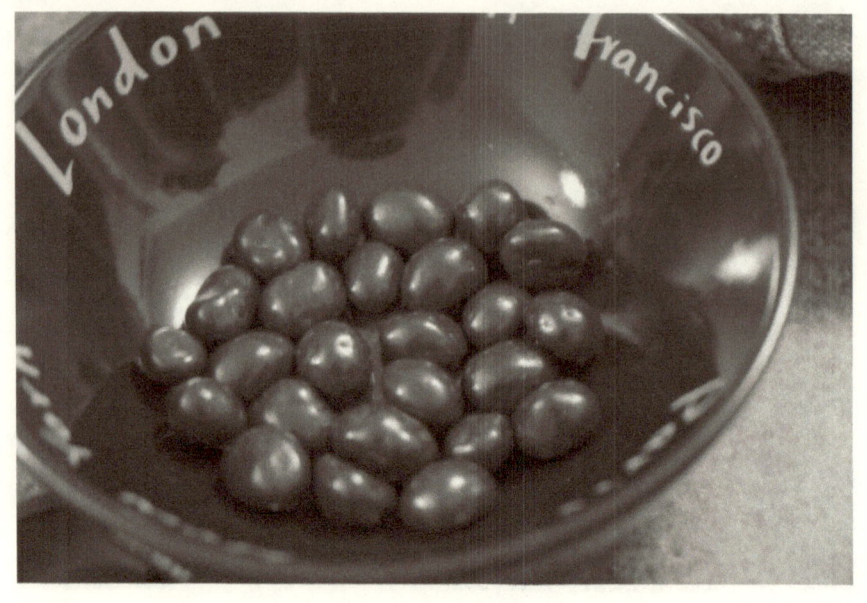

Essential set item:

Chocolate-covered espresso beans

As I mentioned before, this version of the screenplay is from the last draft before we began filming. It was the last draft before I changed it into a shooting script. I have included screenshots for every scene but some inconsistencies may exist between the pictures and the script. I left it like this in order to illustrate how things change in the process of making a film.

When you watch the film you will see how not all changes happen on the set. For instance, during editing I moved part of a scene that takes place between the main character Eddie and his neighbor into a scene between Eddie and the character of Max. Through some creative editing I was able to change the pacing and endings of two scenes with what was written and already filmed.

I believe the script is well written with unique characters, individual voices, and a good story. When comparing the finished product to the script, I realized we filmed the script almost word for word. The compromise I had to make was to make it more dialogue and character based to accommodate the limited budget and time. I think the film turned out fine but if I was to do it again I would have shortened the set-up and gotten the two couples together and interacting sooner. I toned down the humor to keep it closer to a drama and more realistic.

To find out about where you can watch ONE NIGHT go to:

anymomentproductions.com

ONE NIGHT

Screenplay by
Sebastian J. Howley

EXT. CHICAGO SKYLINE-LATE AFTERNOON

The city of Chicago. Establishing.

INT. EDDIE'S APARTMENT-NIGHT

Eddie is on the floor. We move in close to
him as he closes his eyes.

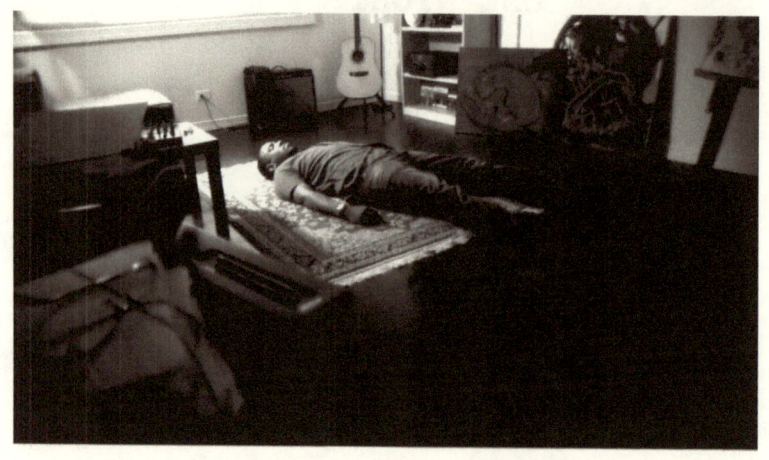

                    EDDIE (V.O.)
        It was one of those nights. One of
        those nights you remember for a
        long, long time. They only come
        around once in a blue moon but can
        make you forget the rest of the
        year in a hurry. That was Nina.
        She put other dames to shame in the
        same way. She could make sour milk
        sweet. She had legs that seemed to
        go on for days...like they would
        never end. Her dress followed her
        curves like water. You'd crawl

across a floor covered in broken glass just to ask: why is there so much broken glass all over the floor? She was my Krpytonite. My one weakness. And it was only a matter of time.

                              DISSOLVE TO:

INT. APARTMENT-FILM NOIR-DREAM SEQUENCE

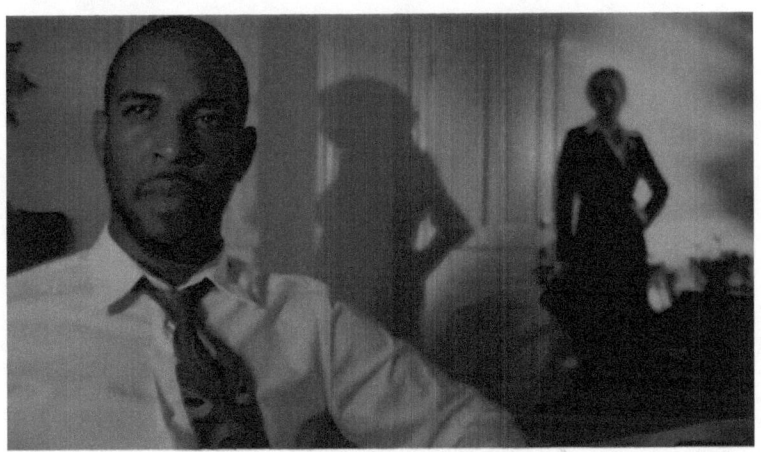

                    EDDIE (V.O.)
I knew one night she would walk through my door and into my life again. My whole universe would come crashing to the ground. Funny thing is, she wouldn't know whether to kiss me or slap me. Honestly, I wouldn't care either way.

              NINA
Eddie?

                    EDDIE
          Who's asking?

                    NINA
          I am. I figured that would be obvious
          since I am the only one here.

                    EDDIE
          Things are not always what they seem,
          dollface.

                    NINA
          Are you saying you're not alone?

          A woman walks out of the bedroom fixing her
          clothes, sees Nina.

                    WOMAN
               (to Eddie)
          You bastard!

          Nina turns and watches her leave.

                    NINA
          I see not much has changed.

                    EDDIE
          Forget about her, I have.

                    NINA
          I knew you didn't really love me.

                    EDDIE
          That was my maid.

          Nina looks around the place, it is a mess.

                    NINA
She's not doing what you're paying
her for. Or maybe she is and
that's why the place hasn't been
cleaned.

                    EDDIE
I see you haven't lost your sense
of humor.

                    NINA
I keep it in my front pocket with
all your empty promises. Cigarette?

                    EDDIE
No thanks, I quit smoking. It's
dangerous.

                    NINA
Are you afraid of danger?

                    EDDIE
Of course not. No real man is.
You know what? I'll take one of
those cigarettes.

                    NINA
Sorry, I can't help you.

                    EDDIE
Why not?

                    NINA
I quit smoking too. Goodbye Eddie.

She turns to leave.

                    EDDIE
What a minute. I said I quit
smoking. I didn't say I quit
beautiful women.

                    NINA
That's your problem. If you really
loved me you would have quit them too.

                    EDDIE
My heart was yours and you know it.
I handed it to you and you tossed
it out on the sidewalk. It got run
over by a librarian who was late
for work.

                    NINA
And who was that red head that was
all over you last night at the
Copa?

                    EDDIE
She was nothing, just working some
angle on me. She tried to sit on
my lap while I was still standing
up. I don't like pushy broads.

                    NINA
Are you trying to tell me
something?

                    EDDIE
Men don't try, they do.

There is a knock on the door.

Nina looks at him.

                    NINA
                   (sad)
          Goodbye Eddie.
                                        CUT TO:

INT. EDDIE'S APARTMENT-DAY

Eddie is on the floor.

A knock at the door.

Eddie opens his eyes.

He sits up.

                    NEIGHBOR (O.S.)
          Eddie, quit daydreaming and open
          the door.

Eddie stands, walks to the door and opens
it.

A young man (NEIGHBOR) stands in the
doorway, holds a globe.

                    NEIGHBOR (CONT'D)
          I think this belongs to you.

Eddie and the neighbor sit on the ground
with the globe between them.

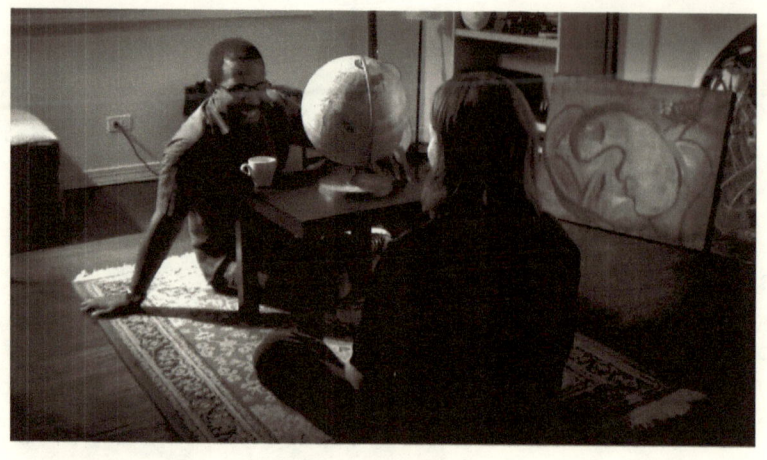

NEIGHBOR
I have some big news.

EDDIE
You're finally getting a hair cut?

NEIGHBOR
No. I'm moving to Los Angeles.

EDDIE
What? You're joking. You almost
had me.

NEIGHBOR
No, no, I'm serious. I'm leaving
in a few days.

EDDIE
I thought you said you'd never set
foot in that city?

NEIGHBOR
I know, I know. A few weeks ago I
was up all night and it just hit

me. I'm sleepwalking through life.
I need to just get out there and
see what happens.

                    EDDIE
That came from staying up one
night?

                    NEIGHBOR
Not just from one night, it was
building up for awhile. A friend
of mine from college who lives in
L.A. called me up and asked me what
I was doing. I had nothing to say.
You know life gives you so many
choices and you have to make a
decision or else you will be stuck
at the fork in the road for the
rest of your life.

                    EDDIE
It does make you want to stay up
every night and try to squeeze the
juice out of life.

                    NEIGHBOR
Squeeze the juice?

                    EDDIE
People say that. What I mean is it
makes me want to just stay up every
night I can.

                    NEIGHBOR
Maybe not every night but life was
meant to be lived.

EDDIE
There is only right now. Isn't
that what you're always saying?

NEIGHBOR
Yes. And it's true. I do say that
all the time but I wasn't listening
to my own advice. I am now.

EDDIE
People are always living in the
past or the future and are really
just stuck somewhere in between.

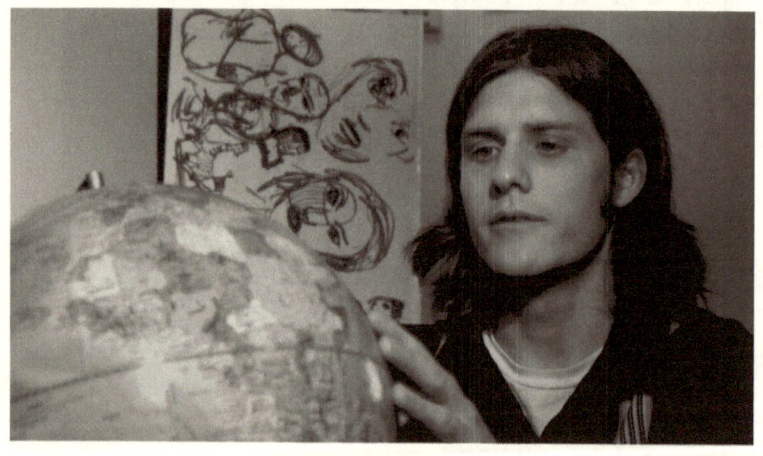

NEIGHBOR
If time is all compressed together
there really only is now. There
never really is tomorrow or
yesterday, or 10 minutes from now.
Look at this globe, it's evening in
Chicago and morning in China but
there's not really a 12 hour
difference. In both places we're
doing what we're doing right now.

And if we spin this thing a
thousand times, whether it's 500
years in the future or a 1000 years
in the past, whatever happens at
those times it all happens in the
present moment.

                    EDDIE
You know that's what I think a lot
of UFOs are. Maybe all the weird things
we see in the sky are just overlapping
images from the future or the past.
It's all layered on top of each other.

                    NEIGHBOR
So you can't put anything off for
tomorrow since tomorrow doesn't exist.

                    EDDIE
Exactly.

                    NEIGHBOR
I'm ready to just start all over.
When I wake up in a few days and
head out West it is going to be a
new me.

                    EDDIE
It sounds like you are ready to get
out there and take over.

                    NEIGHBOR
All I have to do is find a place to
live and a job but how hard could
that be, right? So that's my life,
what are you up to?

                    EDDIE
          Max and I have been working on this
          graphic novel and I think we have
          found someone to help us publish
          it.

Eddie stands up and walks to the table.
He picks up some drawings, walks back,
sits down and hands them to the neighbor.

                    NEIGHBOR
          What are these?

                    EDDIE
          These are some of the main characters.

He holds up a drawing of a female.

                    NEIGHBOR
          She's gorgeous.

                    EDDIE
          She sure is.

The neighbor hands the drawings back to him.

                    NEIGHBOR
          You should come out to California
          for a visit. There is always room
          for another out of work writer out
          in Lalaland.

                    EDDIE
          You know what? I need a change.
          I should throw fate a curve ball.
          I've always wanted to be that guy
          that just hops on a plane and goes
          some place new out of the blue.

Hemingway wasn't afraid of anything.
This is it. Wherever my finger stops
is where I am headed next. That's
where my future will begin.

Eddie spins the globe, puts his finger down
stopping it.

                    NEIGHBOR
          So where is does your future live?

Eddie pulls his finger away from the globe.

His finger lands on:

          CHICAGO.

Eddie scratches his head.

                    EDDIE
          Huh.

                    NEIGHBOR
          It landed on Chicago didn't it?

                    EDDIE
          Apparently I'm not the type of guy
          who just gets on a plane and flies
          somewhere.

                    NEIGHBOR
          Chicago must have unfinished
          business for you, I guess. You
          never know when opportunity will
          knock.

A knock at the door.

The neighbor laughs.

                    EDDIE
          I didn't think you meant literally.
          Come on in.

                    NEIGHBOR
          You aren't going to ask who it is?

                    EDDIE
          I invite danger into my life.

The door opens and Max stands in the hallway
playing with a yo-yo. He holds a large
bouquet of flowers in the other hand.

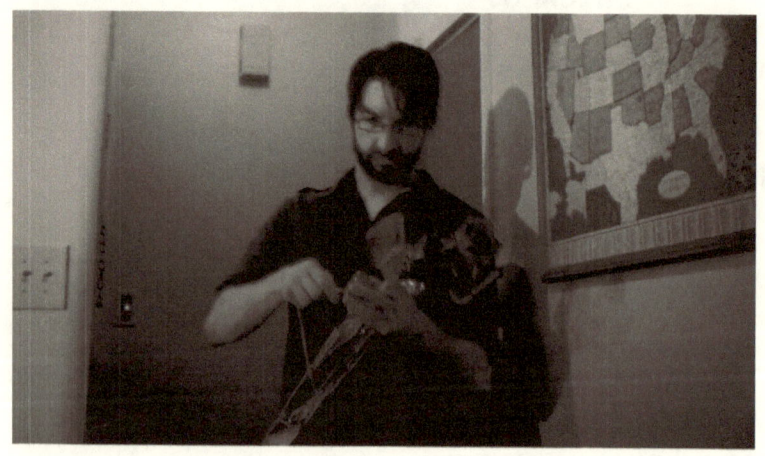

                    NEIGHBOR
          Danger huh?

Eddie shrugs.

                    EDDIE
          Did you find that yo-yo?

                    MAX
        Yes.

                    EDDIE
        That's mine.

Max walks into the apartment and hands him
the yo-yo.

                    MAX
        You guys having a little tea party?

                    EDDIE
        No. We're just talking, drinking
        some tea.

                    MAX
        That's a tea party.

                    NEIGHBOR
        I should get going.

The neighbor stands, Eddie stands also.

                    EDDIE
        Why did you knock Max? You live here.

                    MAX
        I was just checking to see if you
        were still telling people to come
        in without looking to see who it
        was first.

                    NEIGHBOR
            (to Eddie)
        Good luck Eddie.

                    EDDIE
        Thanks.

Eddie and the neighbor shake hands.

                    NEIGHBOR
        Remember Eddie. Life is short,
        don't wait for tomorrow.

                    EDDIE
        I won't.

                    NEIGHBOR
        See you later Max.

                    MAX
        Take it easy.

The neighbor leaves.

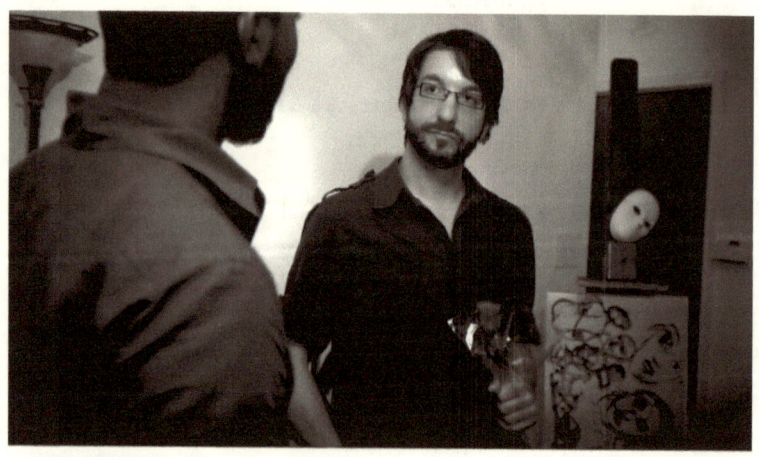

                    EDDIE
        We should really get to work you
        know.

                    MAX
          Let me put these in water first.

Max walks in to the kitchen.

Eddie stays in the living room.

                    EDDIE
          Who are those for?

                    MAX
          Not you.

                    EDDIE
          You have to tell me.

                    MAX
          No I don't.

                    EDDIE
          Yes you do. It's like in a play.
          If you show a gun in the first act
          you have to use it later.

                                        CUT TO:

Max in the kitchen holds a squirt gun. He
fills it with water from the kitchen sink.

Eddie begins to walk in to the kitchen.

Max drops the gun quickly into a drawer and
closes it.

Eddie walks in.

                    EDDIE
          So who are they for?

                    MAX
     No one.

                    EDDIE
     You literally have no choice. You
     have to tell me.

Max pulls the gun out of the drawer and
squirts Eddie.

Eddie doesn't flinch.

                    EDDIE
     That was inappropriate.

EXT. EDDIE'S APARTMENT-LATE AFTERNOON

Max plays his guitar.

Eddie tries to write in a notebook.

Max stops playing.

Eddie tries to write again.

Max begins to play again.

Eddie drops his pen onto the notebook and
sighs.

                              CUT TO:

Eddie and Max throw rubber balls around the
apartment.

They bounce off the walls around them.

                    EDDIE
          That was a hit.

                    MAX
          That didn't even come close to
          hitting me.

                    EDDIE
          Yes it did, you're out.

                    MAX
          Fine.

          Max steps to the side.

          Eddie stands by himself. Looks around.

                    EDDIE
          Ok, you can play again.

                                        CUT TO:

          Eddie sits at the table enjoys a large
          cinnamon roll with a knife and fork.

          He finishes and pushes the plate away.
          He takes the napkin that is tucked into
          his collar off and wipes the corners of
          his mouth. He is pleased with the meal.

          Max walks in.

                    MAX
          Did you just eat my cinnamon roll?

          Eddie stares off, shakes his head.

                              EDDIE
              Cinnamon what?   No...I...no.

                                                    CUT TO:

Max stands at a large tablet of paper
drawing an object.

                              EDDIE
                 It's a dinosaur.   It's a T-Rex.
                 It's the *band* T-Rex.   It's a...

Max slowly stops drawing and turns to Eddie.

                              MAX
                 Playing this game with two people
                 is weird.

                                                    CUT TO:

Max and Eddie are at the table writing.

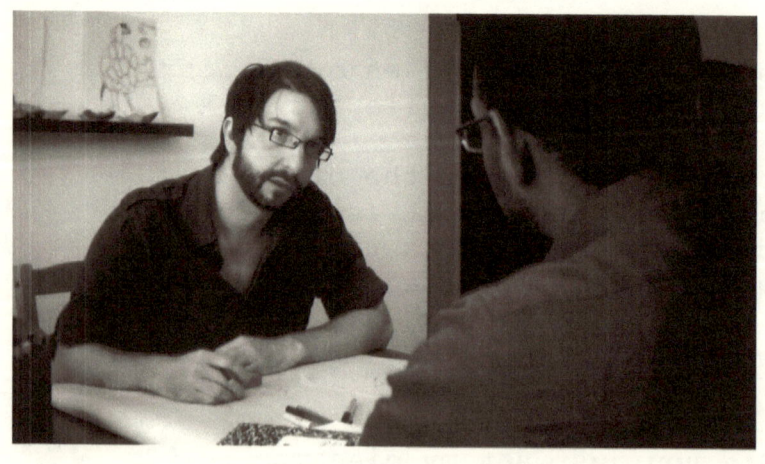

                    EDDIE
I'll have these new pages for you
soon. It'll be about fifty or so
new ones.

                    MAX
Fifty new pages? Are you kidding?

                    EDDIE
No. I can count them if you want.

                    MAX
Eddie how long is this project
going to be? It would have been
easier for me to illustrate the
Bible and the telephone book than
this.

                    EDDIE
That's not a bad idea.

                    MAX
Eddie. I think we should talk
about editing this down to, you
know, something someone might read
someday.

                    EDDIE
You know James Joyce took eleven
years to write Finnegan's Wake and
he said it should take people that
long to read it.

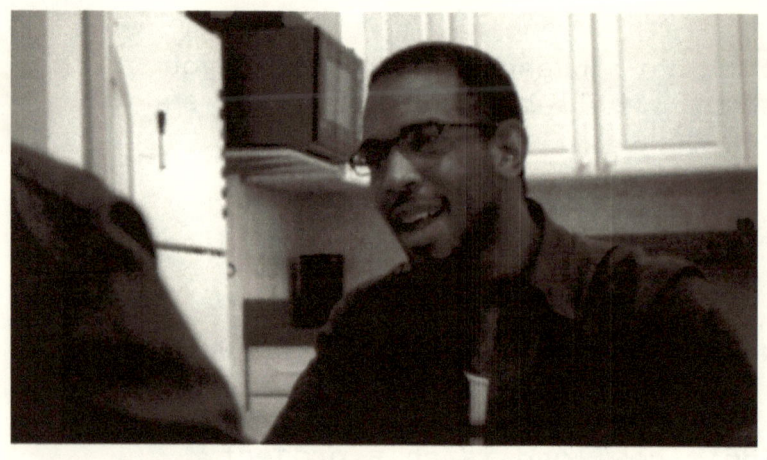

MAX

So now your James Joyce because you
can't stop writing?

EDDIE

What are you getting so worked up
for?

MAX

This started out as a favor and I
want us to work all the time on
stuff. Even get paid for it one
day. But you know I've written one
new song in the last three months
and this thing just keeps getting
longer and longer.

EDDIE

I have a lot to say.

MAX

Eddie we are broke. We bought
three reams of paper and somehow we
are about to run out. We haven't

even finished the story yet. And...
can I be honest?

                    EDDIE
Sure.

Max holds up a sketch.

                    MAX
Is this supposed to be Nina?

                    EDDIE
What? Nina? I copied that out of a
magazine. That's some random model.
I traced that to give you an idea of
what she should look like.

                    MAX
Ok. But it looks like Nina. And I
know you swear up and down that
this is not some obsession project
about her but clearly it is.

                    EDDIE
Just get back to work. You know
all this talking and you could have
finished a page by now.

                    MAX
That would only leave four thousand
more to go. Good for me.

                              CUT TO:

Max draws on the big pad of paper again.

                    EDDIE
It's George Washington crossing the

Mississippi. It's a zombie George
Washington.

Max writes the word zombie on the pad.
Max stops drawing.

                    MAX
          It feels weird again.

                                        CUT TO:

Max walks into the living room with his
guitar. Eddie writes at the table.

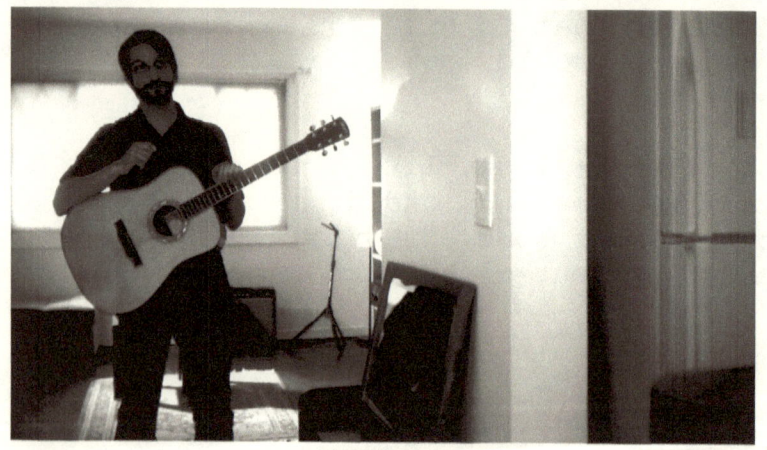

                    MAX
          Were you playing my guitar?

                    EDDIE
          What? No.

                    MAX
          I left it on the guitar stand and I
          just found it on my bed.

                    EDDIE
You're crazy. I know the guitar rule.

                    MAX
Do you? Cause I don't think you do.

                    EDDIE
Well I didn't play it.

                    MAX
I can tell if you did because you're
tone deaf and can't tune a guitar.

                    EDDIE
I didn't play it.

                    MAX
I just have to play one chord that's
it.

                    EDDIE
Go ahead.

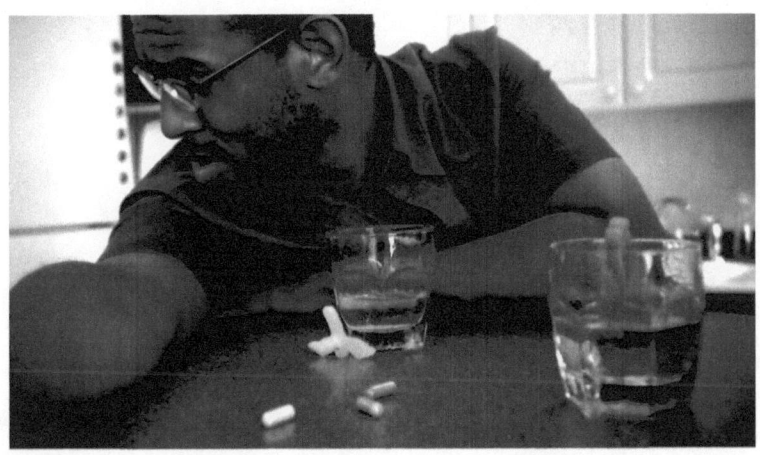

                    MAX
Just tell me you played it and we
can stop all this.

                    EDDIE
I'm not going to lie to make you
happy. Play your little E chord.

                    MAX
I will.

                    EDDIE
Do it. Play two chords. Play a
whole song. I don't care.

Eddie and Max trade stares back and forth.

Max strums the guitar and the horribly out
of tune chord hangs in the air.

Neither move.

                              CUT TO:

 There is a knock on the door.

                    EDDIE
 Come in!

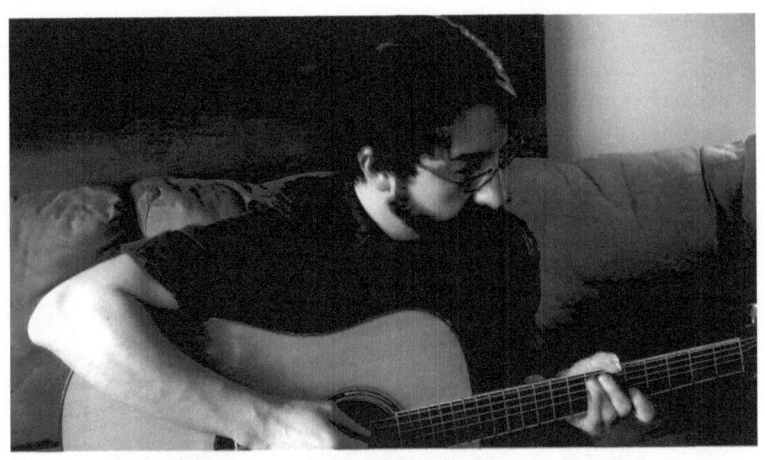

A woman (LANDLORD) walks in.

                    LANDLORD
        You boys haven't packed yet?

                    EDDIE
        Boys?!

                    LANDLORD
        Yes, that's exactly what you are.

                    EDDIE
        You can't kick us out!

                    LANDLORD
        Yes, little boys I can.

                    MAX
        Heh I'm a grown up. Well not all
        the time.

                    EDDIE
        This is crazy.

LANDLORD
I've been telling you for weeks now
to do something about all this and
you haven't done anything.

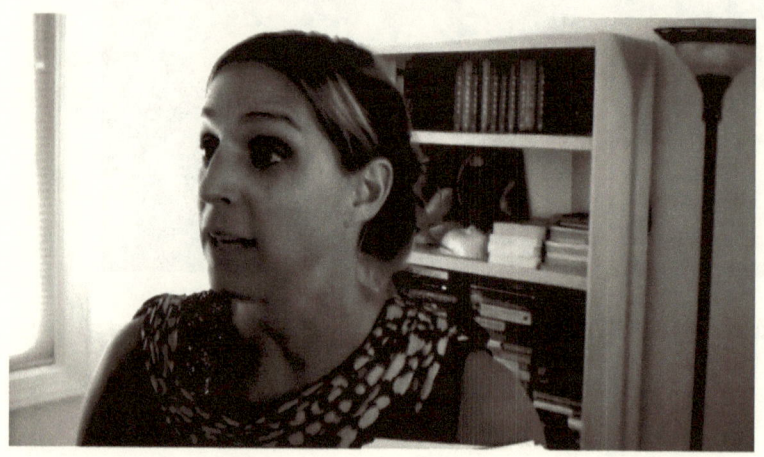

MAX
Weeks?

EDDIE
Listen-

LANDLORD
When was the last time you actually
paid rent?

EDDIE
I told you we were good for it.

LANDLORD
Good for it? What does that mean?
Eddie you're a nice guy but this is
the real world we live in. You have
to find a new place to live and when
you do find a new place to live, I

suggest you actually pay rent. Not
everyone is as nice as I am.

Landlord leaves.

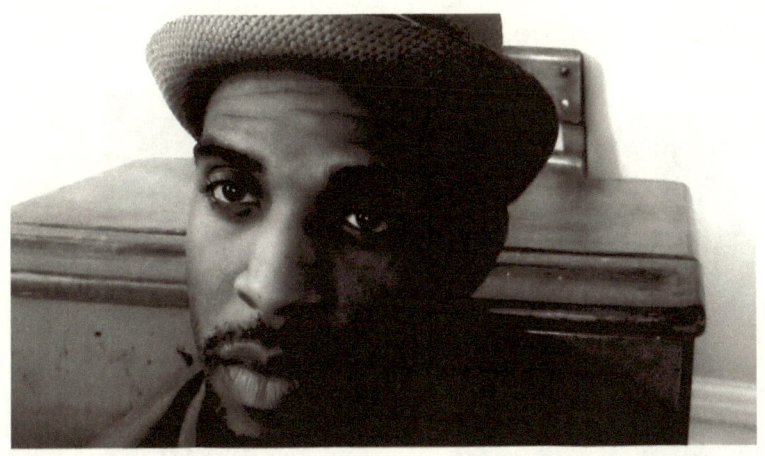

                                        FADE OUT

INT. APARTMENT-DAY LATE

Eddie sits on the couch. He holds a small,
worn, and bent photograph.

The phone rings.

Eddie doesn't move to answer it. The answer
machine picks up.

                    EDDIE'S FATHER (O.S.)
          Eddie. This is your father. You
          have to call about that construction
          job tomorrow. I told them you had
          experience, so use those writing skills
          of yours and make something up. I

pulled a lot of strings for you so
don't blow it kid. Call me after
you call them.

Max walks into the room, holds the flowers.
He is dressed nicely.

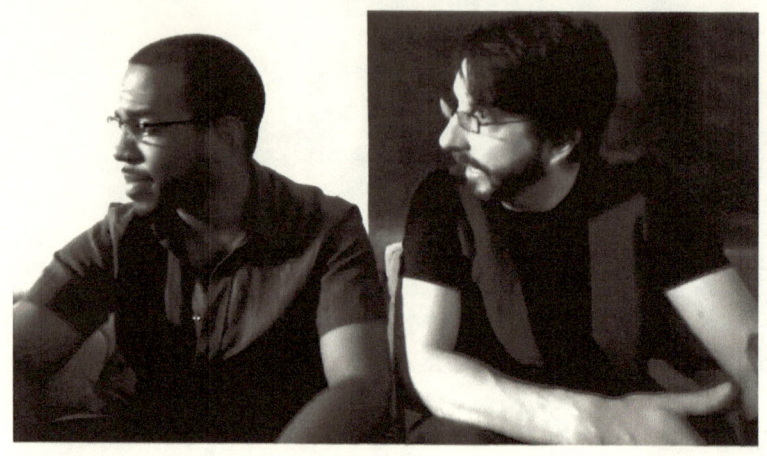

                    MAX
Did the phone just ring?

                    EDDIE
It was nobody. We should be having
a huge party tonight. Tonight should
be a night to remember you know?

                    MAX
I don't think a party is a good idea.

                    EDDIE
I'm starving. Let's get something to
eat at least. Then we can call
people.

Eddie taps the rose Max holds in his hands.

                    EDDIE (CONT'D)
You getting married today?

                    MAX
Not in the mood.

                    EDDIE
Seriously where are you going?

                    MAX
I have a date. I've told you like
a hundred times.

                    EDDIE
No you didn't. I would have
remembered.

                    MAX
Well I have to make it a short
night since I have to come home and
pack and then find a place to stay
until I find a new place to live.

                    EDDIE
She is not going to kick us out
trust me. She has said that a
million times. Has she ever done
it? Ever? No. Remember when we
found that piano in an alley and
tried to hoist it up here and it
fell and crushed that ice cream
cart and almost killed that guy?

                    MAX
That was pretty funny.

                    EDDIE
If she didn't kick us out then she
isn't going to now for not paying
rent for a bit.

                    MAX
What do you mean not paying for a
bit? I thought you said you were
taking care of it?

                    EDDIE
I am. You know Paul at Galaxy
Comics? He knows this dentist that
comes into the store and he told
him about our book. He thought it
sounded good so he agreed to invest
in it and help get it made.

                    MAX
So what does this have to do with
our rent?

                    EDDIE
He agreed to put up half so I have
been saving our rent money. We
have what we need now.

                    MAX
Where am I going to finish doing
the drawings for the book on a park
bench?

                    EDDIE
We can get this made and we can
make money doing what we want to do
our way. Paul already said he
would sell it at the store.

                    MAX
So you still have all the money?

                    EDDIE
Yes. If you think my plan won't
work we can give her the money and
start from scratch. She's not
going to kick us out.

Max gets up and walks to the front door.
He opens the door to leave. There is an
eviction notice taped to the door.

                    MAX
I don't think she is letting us off
the hook this time Eddie.

                    EDDIE
She doesn't mean that.

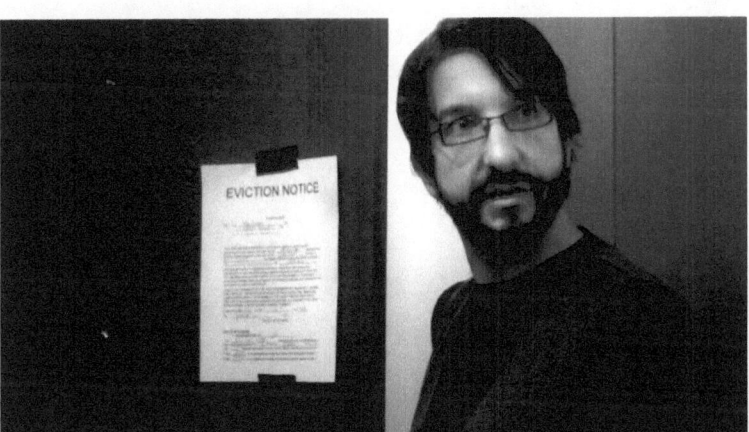

                    MAX
Are you insane? Listen I have to go.

                    EDDIE
          What am I going to do tonight?

                    MAX
          Pack your stuff.

                    EDDIE
          I'm going to get something to eat.
          I'll walk with you.

                    MAX
          Ok but you have to leave before she
          gets there.

Eddie gets up and heads to his room.

Eddie comes back out, he holds two ties in
his hands.

                    EDDIE
          Which one do you like better?

EXT. STREET-EVENING

Eddie and Max walk down the street.

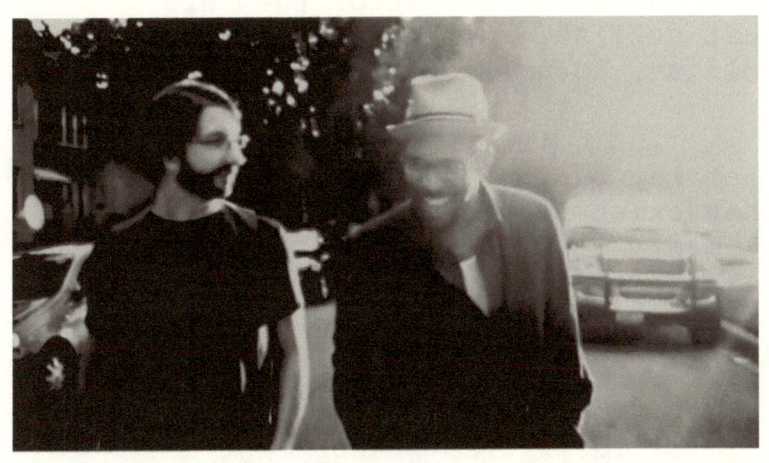

                    MAX
        If we ever finish your book we
        should create a superhero.

                    EDDIE
        You mean with superpowers and
        everything?

                    MAX
        Yeah.

                    EDDIE
        Every superpower is just some form
        of perverted narcissism.

                    MAX
        All of them?

                    EDDIE
        All of them except Superman's

indestructibility. He had all them together. That's smart. You're supposed to have superpowers to help the world. Most of them are just selfish. All of them are just selfish, actually.

                MAX
That may be your problem. Who says they exist for the benefit of others?

                EDDIE
Are you insane? They have those gifts to make all of us better and to stop us from ruining ourselves. They are different so they can teach us to realize our potential and save us from...stuff. Godzilla came from nuclear bombs, his powers...his whole being is a warning to us.

                MAX
So just because someone can fly that means they have to save the world?

                EDDIE
Yes. But not just flying. Flying. Flying is the worst. Everyone wants to fly. You can fly in a plane or a helicopter or a hang glider, flying is redundant. X-ray vision makes no sense also. So you can see through something? What if you get shot? A lot of help you'd be. And forget about invisibility.

That's the worst of them all. You give ten guys invisibility and they would be hanging out in some dressing room at the mall or in a women's locker room somewhere. Not one of them would try to save the world. See that's why female super heroes are practical. Wonder Woman's jet was invisible not her. Stealth, now that's smart. And her bullet proof wrist bracelets? She could really get the job done.

                    MAX
Yeah.

They walk for a bit.

                    MAX (CONT'D)
Having said that, if you could have any superpower what would it be?

                    EDDIE
Invisibility.

                    MAX
Yeah. Me too.

Eddie and Max stop walking, stand on a corner.

                              FADE OUT

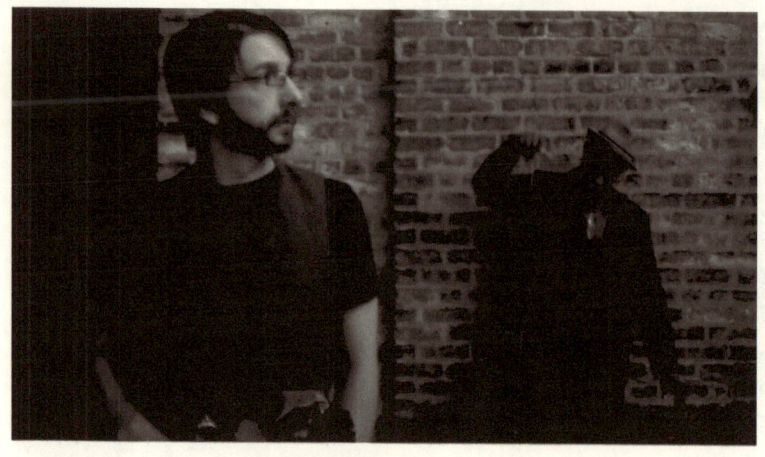

                    EDDIE
I think you may have been stood up
my friend.

                    MAX
No, she's just late.

                    EDDIE
I'm starving Max.

                    MAX
Then go. I'm a big boy.

                    EDDIE
I can't just let you meet her by
yourself. I can be your out. If
she walks up and your first thought
is to run then we can use a code
word and I can be your excuse to
leave her standing on this corner.

                    MAX
A code word?

                    EDDIE
          Yeah, like...timpani.

                    MAX
          Timpani? How am I going to use
          that in a sentence?

                    EDDIE
          That was just my first thought.

                    MAX
          You live in a dark world you know
          that?

                    EDDIE
          I live in the real world.

                    MAX
          I'm going to go try to call her.

Max walks away. Eddie stands by himself for
a moment.

Veronica walks up.

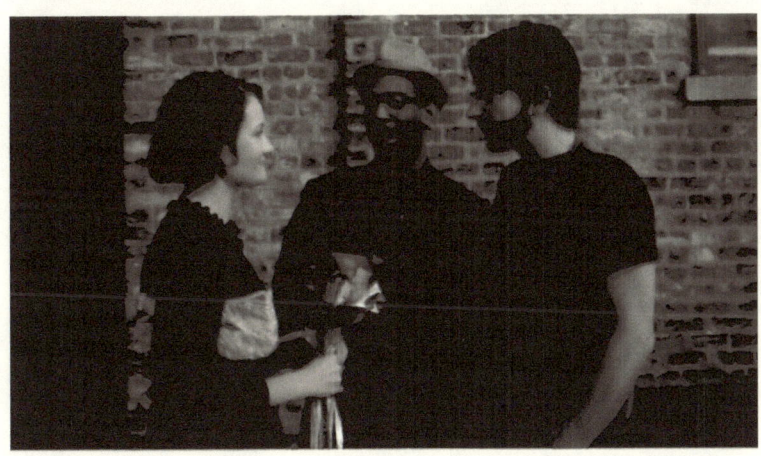

                    VERONICA
     I am so sorry I am late. Wow, you
     look totally different than I
     pictured you. But that's good. Do
     I look how you pictured me?

                    EDDIE
     No I-

                    VERONICA
     That's ok. I'm not saying it's a
     bad thing. I just a little nervous-

Max walks up. Eddie sees him and grabs his
shoulder.

                    EDDIE
     This is Max.

                    VERONICA
     Oh ok. Wow. I'm sorry.

                    MAX
     Great to finally meet you.

He hands her the flowers and hugs her.

                    VERONICA
     These are lovely.

She leans forward and hugs Eddie too.

                    EDDIE
          (to Max, quietly)
     Timpani. Timpani.

VERONICA

That was really sweet to bring
your friend. Make me feel at ease
in a group. Really sweet of you.

MAX

No, no he was just waiting with me.
He has a lot to do tonight.

VERONICA

Like what?

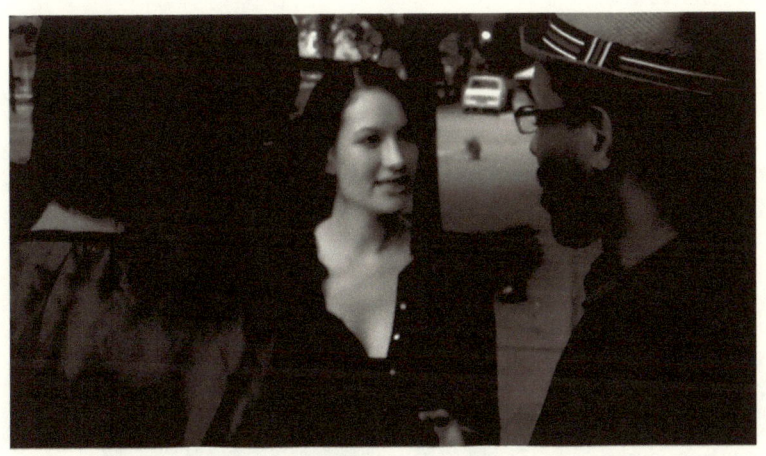

MAX

He has-

EDDIE

I was going to get something to
eat, then-

VERONICA

Then just eat with us. Come on, it
will be fun. Max, I can get to know
you better with your best friend
with us. Let's go.

Veronica walks away.

Max stares at Eddie.

                    EDDIE
                (smiles)
            You're my best friend.

                    MAX
            Have an appetizer and then you have
            to leave.

INT. RESTAURANT-NIGHT

Eddie, Max, and Veronica sit in awkward
silence.

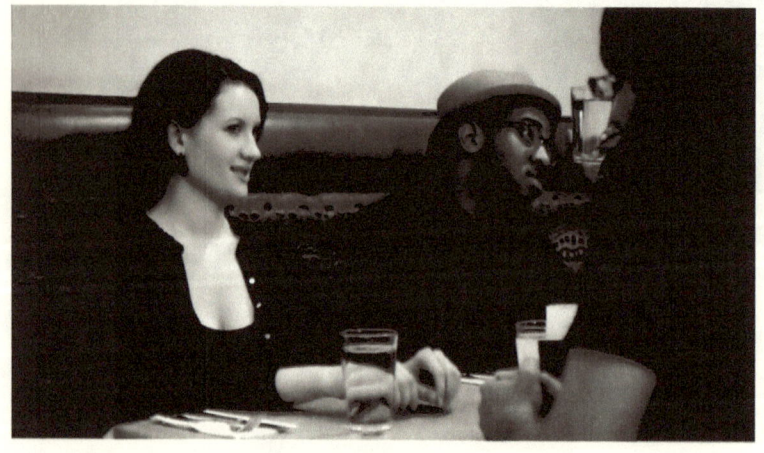

                    VERONICA
            Did you know that the only thing
            that separates humans from animals
            is the use of condiments?

Max tilts his head.

                    MAX
          Interesting. Did you know that
          Edward?

                    EDDIE
          I did not.

                    VERONICA
          Yep.

                    EDDIE
          Was that from a book you read or
          something? What happens if they
          find an animal using condiments?
          Would that mean there is no difference
          between us humans and the animals?

                    VERONICA
          I was actually just making a joke.

                    EDDIE
          Oh. Of course.

The waitress comes up the table.

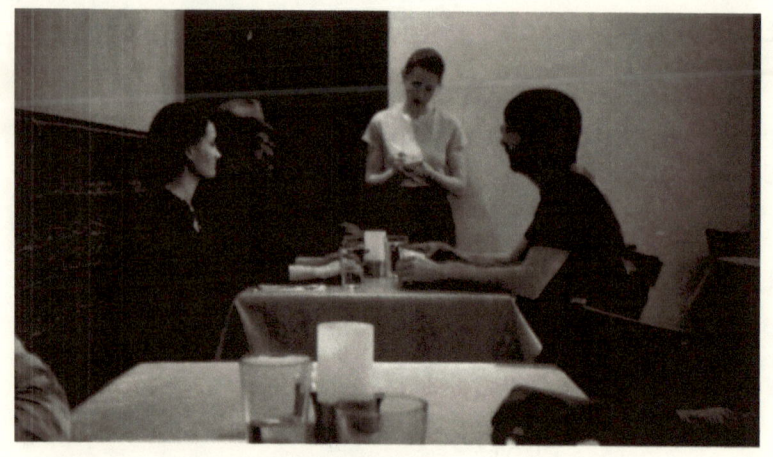

                    WAITRESS
         Are we all set?

                    EDDIE
         We sure are.

Veronica shrugs and then shakes her head
'no.'

                    WAITRESS
         Ok, I'll be back.

Eddie sighs.

                    MAX
         What?

                    EDDIE
         That was our chance to order.
         Everyone knows if you don't order
         the first time they come to the
         table they just let you sit there
         forever.

                    MAX
I don't think either of us is in
a hurry right now.

                    EDDIE
This is true.

                    VERONICA
You guys are funny. You're like
an old married couple. I love it.

                    MAX
We have known each other for a
long, long time.

                    VERONICA
That's great. I don't have any old
friends, you know? I moved here all
by myself to start over again. I
am doing really well too. But it
is kind of tough to not know
anyone. But if I hadn't moved here
where I don't know anyone then I
wouldn't have met you two because I
would have already known people. But
then again if I hadn't moved here I
wouldn't have met you either because
I would have moved somewhere else.

Max and Eddie nod in agreement but are
slightly confused.

                    MAX
     Exactly.

The waitress returns.

                    WAITRESS
          I hope I wasn't gone too long. Did
          you have any questions?

                    EDDIE
          I do. Have you ever seen a monkey
          use ketchup?

                    WAITRESS
          Any intelligent questions?

                    MAX
          Three slices of cheese pizza please
          and a pitcher of orange soda.

The waitress walks away.

                    VERONICA
                    (to Max)
          What's your favorite artificial
          flavor?

                    EDDIE
          Grape.

                    MAX
          I'm partial to orange.

                    VERONICA
          Me too. Movie theater seats?

                    EDDIE
          Center aisle, seats in the middle.

                    MAX
          Side and close up so you can slouch
          down.

                    VERONICA
And get comfy. Exactly. Crossword,
Sudoku or word jumble.

                    EDDIE
Word jumble.

                    MAX
Crossword.

                    VERONICA
Indeed. We have a lot in common.

                    EDDIE
Wow you guys should really go on a
date sometime.

Max looks at Eddie.

                    EDDIE (CONT'D)
I'm just saying.

                    VERONICA
This place reminds me of the pizza
place I used to go to in college.
We lived there. Literally. I mean
we had the apartment upstairs. We
used to go there and study. It's
so sad because one of my friends who
still lives there said it went out of
business.

                    EDDIE
That reminds me. I found this
notebook the other day and I can't
remember anything about it. It's
from my freshman year in college
and I don't recognize it at all. I

don't remember the classes, the
notes, or anything. Who was this
person? It makes me feel a little
crazy. I used to sleepwalk and
it's the same thing you know? Who
was steering the ship then?

                    MAX
I ask myself that same question
about you when you are awake.

Veronica chuckles.

Eddie pulls out a little notebook.

                    EDDIE
Anyway, the weirdest thing is the
daily to-do list I used to make.
They all start with an entry for
breakfast. Was there really a time
in my life when I needed a daily
to-do list that started with an
entry for breakfast? Who was this
person?

Eddie flips through the little notebook.
He stops on a page that has been half torn
out. His face is filled with sadness.

                    MAX
        What is it?

                    EDDIE
        Nothing.

Eddie closes the notebook.

                    MAX
        That's a mighty nothing. Something
        about Nina I presume?

                    EDDIE
        It was nothing. Trust me.

                    MAX
        Why don't you just call her or
        better yet, throw away that
        notebook. Which, if I may be
        honest, is the real reason you are
        still carrying around that
        notebook.

                    EDDIE
You are so wise Maximillian. Wise
beyond your years.

                    MAX
I'm being serious. Let Nina go.

                    EDDIE
There's nothing to let go of.
Look, it's just a torn page. I
already let go of it obviously,
it's torn out. Whatever it was.

                    VERONICA
Who's Nina? If you don't mind me
asking.

                    EDDIE
She was someone. Now she doesn't
exist. She disappeared before my very
eyes.

                    VERONICA
               (quietly)
She died?

Veronica turns to Max.

Max shakes his head "no" to her.

Eddie stares off.

The food is served by the waitress.

                    WAITRESS
Anything else?

                    EDDIE
     Yes.

                    CUSTOMER (O.S.)
     M'am.

Waitress holds her hand up to the next
table.

                    WAITRESS
     Just a second.

                    EDDIE
     Where's the bathroom?

                    WAITRESS
     It's in the back but you need the
     key from the front counter.

Waitress starts to walk away.

                    EDDIE
     Wait! A key from the counter?

She stops.

                    WAITRESS
     Yes. Everyone does it.

                    EDDIE
     No offense but I'm not interested
     in what other people are doing. I
     want to wash my hands so I can eat,
     I don't want to carry some dirty
     frisbee with a key attached to it
     before I eat. What are we in a gas
     station?

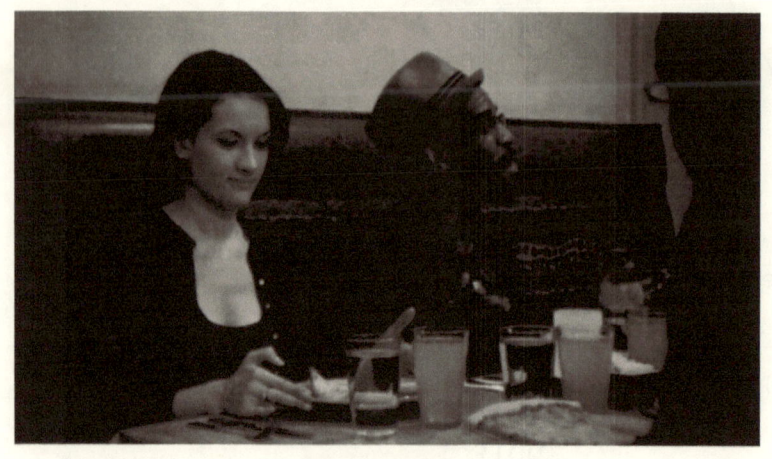

                    WAITRESS
        That's just the way it is.

                    EDDIE
        Can you go back there and open the
        door for me?

                    WAITRESS
        No your highness I can't.

                    EDDIE
        It's your key you open it.

                    WAITRESS
        I can open the front door for you
        if you want.

                    EDDIE
        I'm sorry. We got off on the wrong
        foot. Let me just ask you something.
        Why do you really have a key?

                    MAX
        Eddie.

                    WAITRESS
The bathrooms are for paying
customers only.

                      MAX
Be cool Eddie.

                    EDDIE
So you can keep homeless people
out, oh I see. Make people use a
key and they're homeless so they
don't have keys and they'll get
confused and can't use your
precious bathrooms.

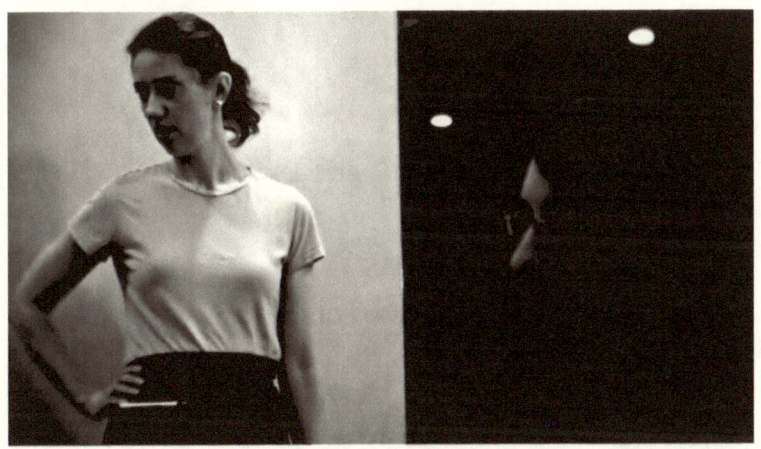

                    WAITRESS
Listen, we have the right to refuse
service to anyone.

                    EDDIE
No you don't.

The waitress picks up his piece of pizza.

                    MAX
     Wait!

The waitress stops.

                    MAX (cont'd)
     He's sorry.   He's had a bad day.
     We promise he will be good.

The waitress stares at Eddie then puts his
piece of pizza back on the table.

Eddie watches her walk away as Max stares
him down.

EXT. RESTAURANT-NIGHT-LATER

                    EDDIE
     So what movie are you seeing?

                    MAX
          (sternly)
     Eddie. Don't you have packing to
     do?

                    EDDIE
     I'm just asking. I haven't been
     to the Fullerton in awhile.

                    VERONICA
     I don't think you will anytime soon
     either.

                    EDDIE
     Why?

                         VERONICA
          It burned down last week.

Max and Eddie stop walking.

                           EDDIE
             It what?

                         VERONICA
          Yeah. Is that where we were
          headed? It's gone boys. The
          owner's in jail, it's like an
          insurance fraud thing. Didn't you
          hear those hundred fire trucks last
          Friday?

Max and Eddie shrug.

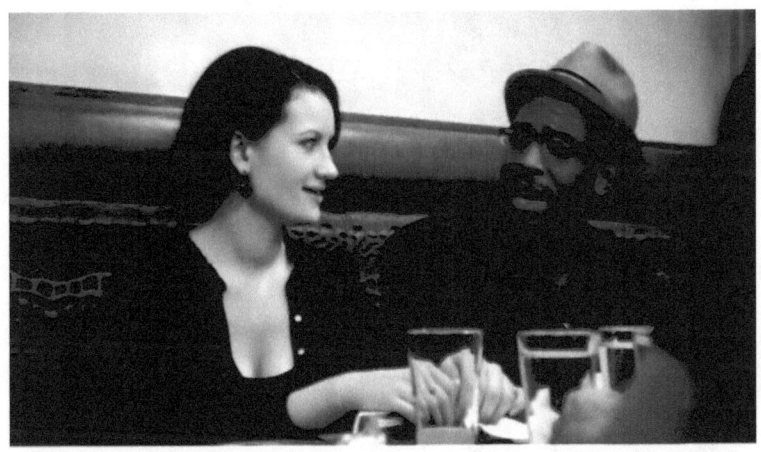

                          EDDIE
          Well this is depressing.
          I loved that old theater.

                        VERONICA
          I love that old movie theater

smell. If I ever made a cologne
it would smell like a movie
theater. A little popcorn, a hint
of junior mints. You know what I'd
call it? Matinee.

Eddie and Max look at Veronica.

                    VERONICA
We can just go to a different
theater.

                    EDDIE
You seem like a nice person but
that's like saying, "don't worry
about that old person dying, you
can just get another grandpa."

                    VERONICA
This theater was like your Grandpa?

                    MAX
He gets emotional about things.

                    VERONICA
We should go to my roommate's
party. That would be so much more
fun that seeing a movie. You like
to have fun don't you Eddie?

                    EDDIE
I guess.

                    MAX
Eddie has to get going. He has all
this work to do. Not just physical
work but spiritual work. Deep
complex work inside himself.

                    VERONICA
Seriously?

                    MAX
Yes. Seriously.

                    VERONICA
He should still come to the party.
We have them all the time but
tonight it's for my roommate's
birthday. We can go to the movies
any night. This party is only
happening one night.

                    EDDIE
I thought you just said they throw
them all the time?

                    VERONICA
They do but this particular party
only happens once. It can't be
repeated. Don't you want to live
life Eddie?

                    EDDIE
I guess. Why are you so concerned
about me?

                    VERONICA
Your aura is a confused mess right
now. It's all cluttered. You have
to let the energy flow more. It's
all bottled up, right here.

She points at his heart.

Eddie looks down and she hits his nose.

                    VERONICA (CONT'D)
        Not really but parties are fun.
        Let's go.

Veronica gets up and walks away. Max shrugs
to Eddie.

INT. SIDEWALK-NIGHT

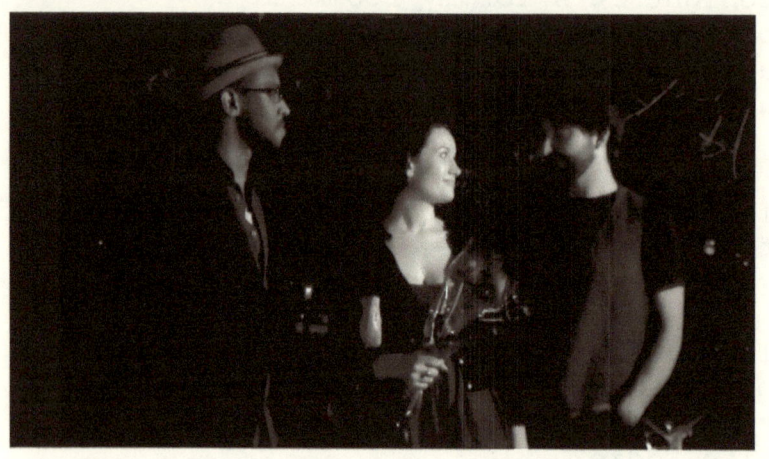

                    EDDIE
        You know this party should set the
        tone for the night. Let's not look
        at tonight like it's a funeral.
        Let's have fun.

                    VERONICA
        You're ready to have fun now?

                    EDDIE
        I'm always ready.

                    VERONICA
I doubt that.

                    MAX
                (to Eddie)
What do you have in mind?

                    EDDIE
Let's stay up all night and watch
the sunrise.

                    VERONICA
That's an excellent idea.

                    MAX
If you buy a ticket to the Eddie
express you may not be happy with
where it takes you.

                    VERONICA
We can get off anytime we want.
Oh, that sounded weird.

                    EDDIE
Seriously. We are going to hang out
all night and have some fun.
Packing can take ten minutes.

                    VERONICA
What are you packing?

                    EDDIE
Nothing. Are we all agreed?

                    VERONICA
It's a plan.

INT. VERONICA'S APARTMENT-NIGHT

Max and Eddie stand watching people.

                    MAX
          Doesn't that girl look like Nina?

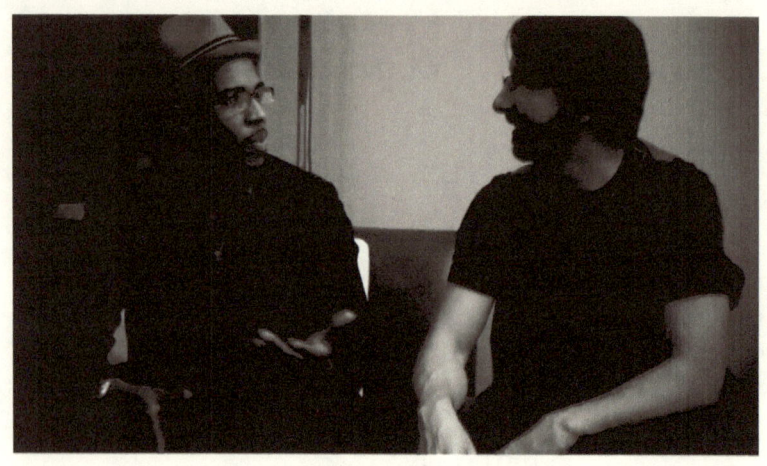

                    EDDIE
          No, not really. Thanks for
          mentioning it though.

                    MAX
          You didn't even look.

                    EDDIE
          I know.

                    MAX
          Why?

                    EDDIE
          Fear.

                    MAX
You're really not over her yet are
you?

                    EDDIE
Sure I am. I've been over her for
like hours now.

                    MAX
I really think that's her.

                    EDDIE
What do you want me to do about it?

                    VERONICA
You guys want to dance?

                    EDDIE
I'm going to camp out here on the
couch.

                    VERONICA
Booooooo.

Michelle, Veronica's roommate, walks up to
them.

                    MICHELLE
You came back already? I told you
he'd be a loser.

                    VERONICA
No. He's right here.

Veronica points to Max.

                    MICHELLE
Oh, I'm sorry. Hi!

                    VERONICA
          This is Max and this is Eddie.

Eddie waves from the couch.

Michelle sits down next to Eddie.

                    MICHELLE
          Nice to meet you.

                    EDDIE
          Nice to meet you.

                    MICHELLE
          We weren't sure whether we should
          have the party or not with
          everything going on.

                    EDDIE
          Going on with what?

                    MICHELLE
          You know. The war.

                    EDDIE
          Oh. Which war?

                    MICHELLE
          Exactly. The whole world is in
          trouble right now.

                    EDDIE
          No, I mean what war?

Michelle stares at him.

                              CUT TO:

Max and Veronica stand by the wall.
It has framed photos hanging up.

                    MAX
        I like your place alot.

                    VERONICA
        Thank you.

                    MAX
        Who did these photos?

                    VERONICA
        I did.

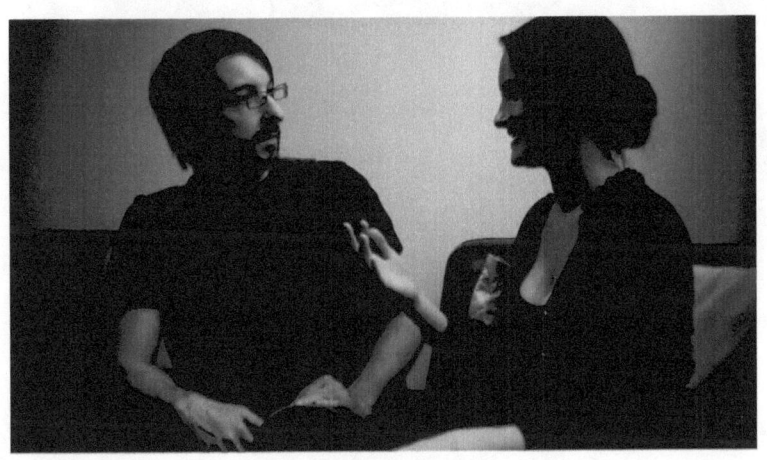

                    MAX
        These are great.

                    VERONICA
        Thank you. I need to start taking
        new ones. These are old. I haven't
        figured out what my new project
        should be.

The photos are of various subjects. Max
points to a photo of Paris.

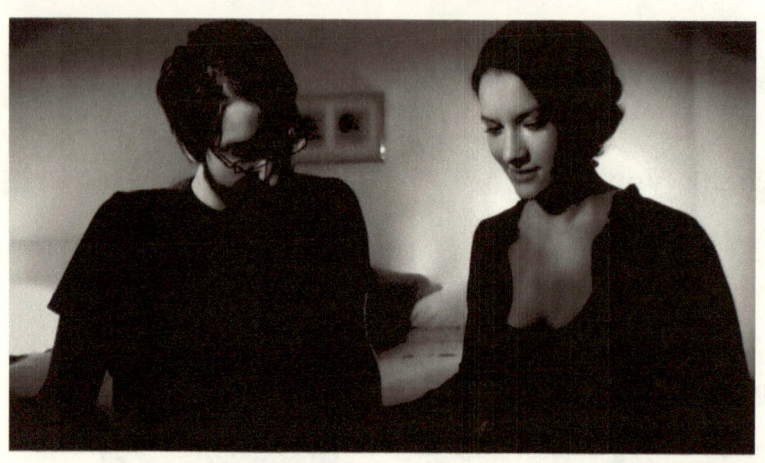

                    MAX
When were you in Paris?

                    VERONICA
Four years ago.

                    MAX
I was too.

                    VERONICA
No.

                    MAX
Yes.

                    VERONICA
That's odd.

                         CUT TO:

Eddie sits on the couch next to Michelle.

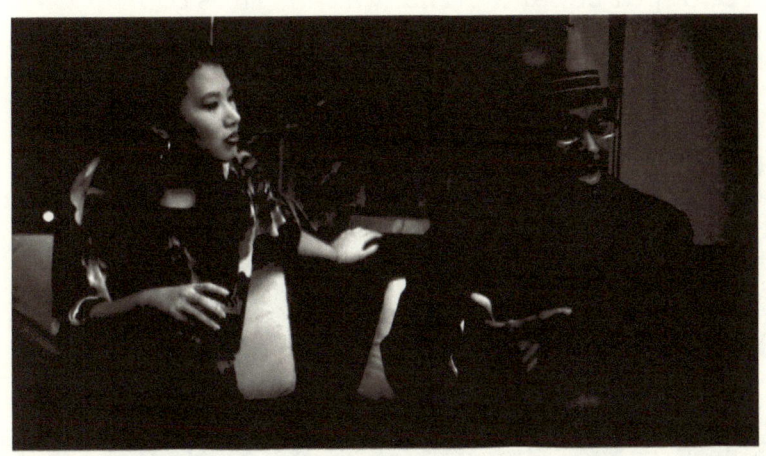

                    EDDIE
I've heard the leader of Iran before
and North Korea but I don't know the
exact names of their leaders. I do
remember there was a character in the
Eighties called the Silent Sheik and
he battled the X-Force in an eight
issue mini-series. I think he was
from Iran.

Michelle just stares at him.

                    MICHELLE
Oh ok. You know I have to go see
how the drink situation is and I'm
being rude to some of my guests.
I'll talk to you in a little bit ok?

Michelle gets up and walks away.

Eddie stares off into the crowd. The loud
music fades away.

The crowd parts and Nina walks in slow
motion towards him.

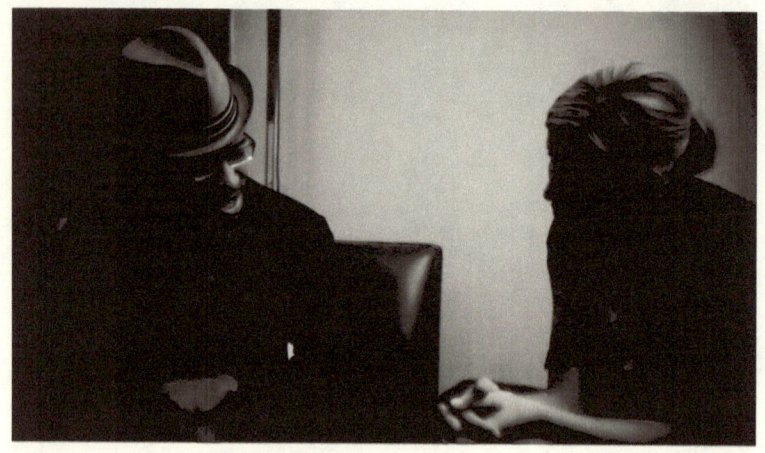

                    NINA
        Eddie. Eddie.

Eddie doesn't respond.

                    NINA
        Eddie?!

Eddie snaps out of it. He realizes she is
actually standing in front of him and he is
not daydreaming.

                    NINA (cont'd)
        What are you doing? I've been
        standing here in front of you for
        like ten minutes.

                    EDDIE
        I was...I don't know where I was
        then. I know you won't believe me

but I'm not angry with you.

Nina recoils.

                    NINA
What does that mean?

                    EDDIE
I don't know what that was supposed
to mean. I guess I was trying to
say I'm happy to see you.

                    NINA
Why not just say that?

                    EDDIE
This is not how I pictured this
moment.

Nina turns and walks away.

Eddie follows her.

                    EDDIE
Nina. Please. Give me a minute.

Nina stops walking.

                    EDDIE
Please. Can we talk somewhere
quieter?

                                    CUT TO:

Eddie and Nina stand in the bathroom.

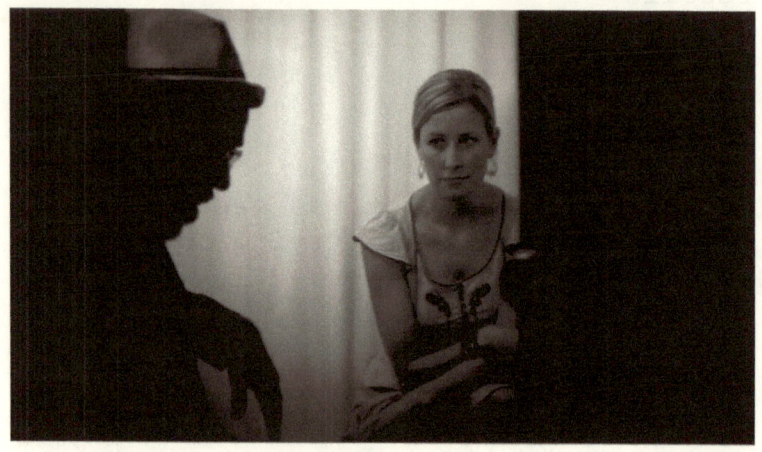

                    NINA
You've been playing out this scene
in your head over and over I bet.

                    EDDIE
No I haven't I-mean in some way. I
knew I would see you again. I hoped
I would see you again.

                    NINA
You know this isn't one of your
little stories. This is real life.
You don't get to rehearse or pick
exactly what to say.

Eddie takes a step closer to her.

                    EDDIE
We should talk and this isn't the
place.

                    NINA
It wouldn't help either of us.

                    EDDIE
Don't you ever miss us?

                    NINA
Sometimes. Sometimes I wish we
could go back and start all over
again.

                    EDDIE
You do?

                    NINA
Sometimes. What are you doing with
yourself now?

                    EDDIE
I'm...I'm great. Max and I have a
book we are putting together and we
have some offers for it. I'm
writing a lot. I am going to have
to look in to some rental properties
soon too. Things are picking up.

                    NINA
Seriously?

                    EDDIE
Yes. We should hang out sometime.
Be in each other's lives. As friends,
then maybe, maybe one day more.

                    NINA
That would never work, we both know
that. We'd both just be acting like
nothing happened. It's over Eddie.

Someday we can be friends again I
just need time.

                    EDDIE
Nina, do something crazy.

                    NINA
Like what?

                    EDDIE
Stay up with us all night. We're
going to watch the sun rise.

                    NINA
I have to be at work tomorrow
morning Eddie. Don't you have to
work?

                    EDDIE
Not tomorrow. No.

                    NINA
Well I do.

                    EDDIE
It's the right thing to do.

                    NINA
Why?

                    EDDIE
Because life is short. We might
not get another night to spend
together.

                    NINA
Eddie. I'm not just going to walk
around all night with you.

EDDIE

We are alive right now. We should
enjoy every sunrise and sunset. We
have no idea how many we have left.

NINA

Are you drunk?

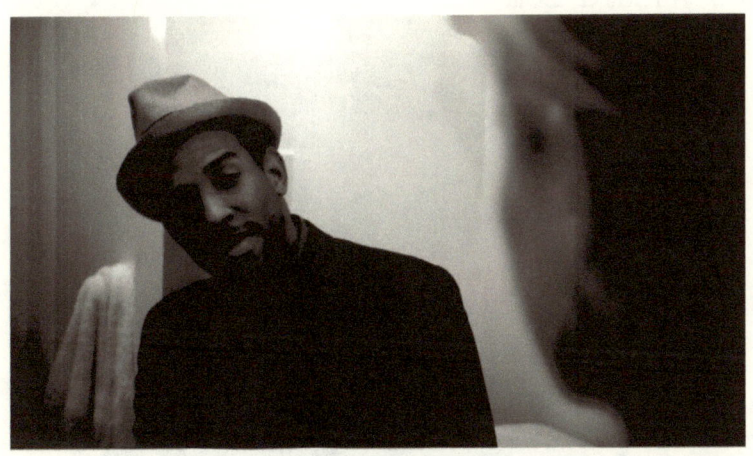

EDDIE

No. I'm not drunk or crazy. What
do you have to lose? Honestly. We
have known each other for almost
our entire lives. We have shared
so many amazing moments and some
really horrible ones too. No one
on this planet knows me better than
you. No one. I know it sounds
crazy but it could also be one of
those nights we talk about years
later. One of those nights that
only happen once in a long, long
while. If we have a boring or bad
night than the worst thing that

happens is you are tired tomorrow and we never see each other again. But if tonight is amazing than we can make it right between us. If you don't think about us and have anything to say to me than I will understand but if you even occasionally think about us then you should come too.

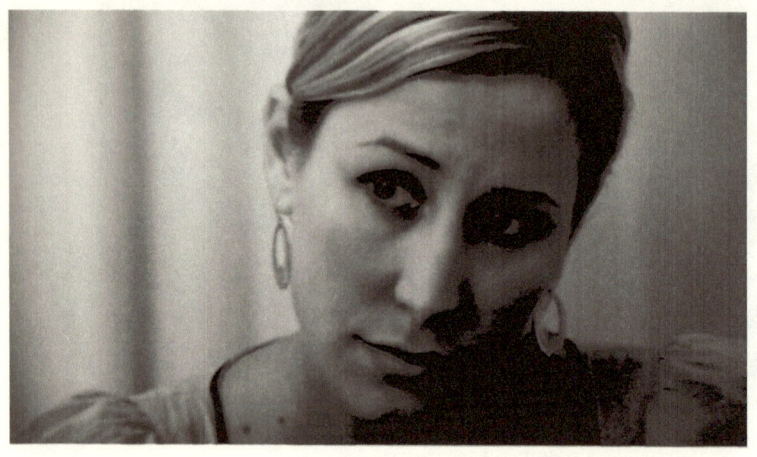

                              FADE OUT:

Eddie and Nina walk up to Max and Veronica. Max looks at Nina and smiles. He flashes a look at Eddie, both hopeful and confused.

The music is very loud.

                    MAX
I bet you two have alot to talk about.

                    NINA
Do I like chocolate?

                    MAX
No you two...never mind. It's nice
to see you.

                    NINA
It's nice to see you too.

                    MAX
It's kind of hard to talk here.

                    EDDIE
               (to Nina)
Do you want to go somewhere?

                    NINA
Ok.

Eddie looks at Max.

                    EDDIE
               (to Max)
I guess I will see you later.

                    VERONICA
You're leaving? I thought we were
going to stay together and watch
the sunrise? I thought we were a
team?

                    MAX
If he wants to leave that's ok.

                    VERONICA
I'm going to go get my camera.
Tonight is going to be my new
photo project.

Veronica walks away quickly.

Eddie leans toward Max.

                    EDDIE
          You don't have to go with us. It's
          ok.

Veronica returns with a camera bag.

                    VERONICA
          Let's go!

EXT. EDDIE/MAX'S APARTMENT-NIGHT

The door opens.

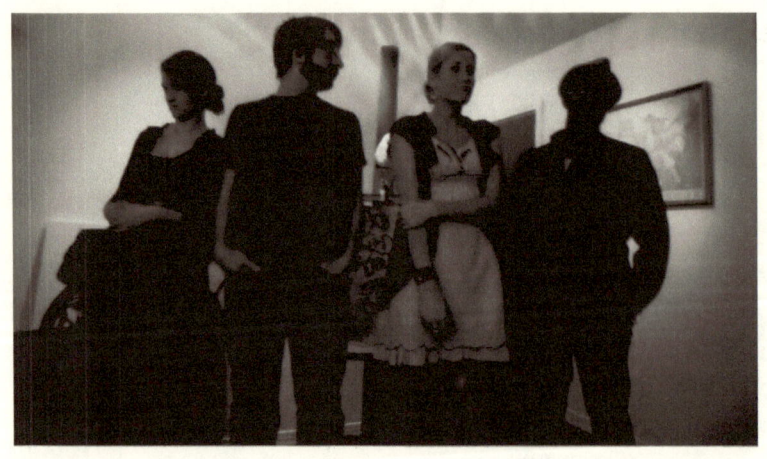

                    NINA
          This place hasn't really changed
          has it?

Nina walks over to the school desk.

                    NINA (CONT'D)
        Is this from our old school?

                    EDDIE
        Yes. They were throwing them
        out. That's my old desk.

He lifts the lid.

Inside it says "I love Nina."

                    NINA
        Wow. That's sweet and creepy all
        at the same time.

                    EDDIE
        It's not creepy. They were going
        to throw them away.

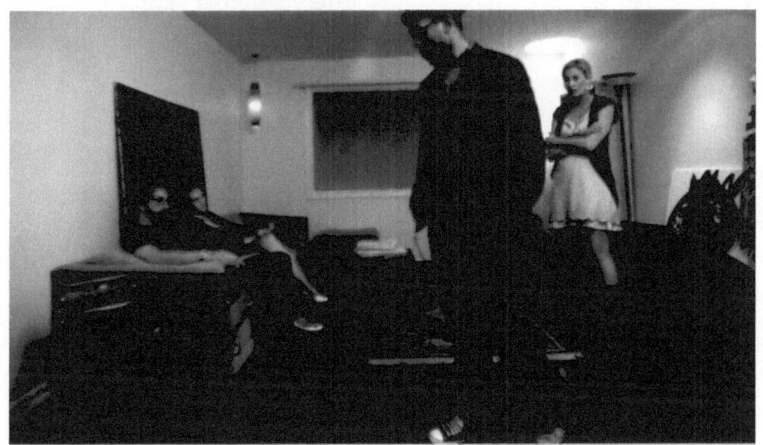

The middle of the room has a model of the
planets hanging from the ceiling with wire.
Nina walks over to it.

The wall is covered in children's art.

                    NINA
Who's art is this?

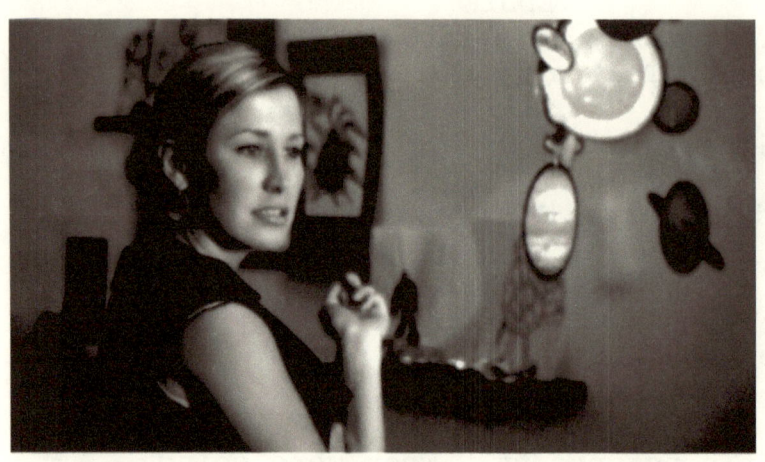

                    MAX
          My niece and nephew. They send me
          stuff almost everyday.

                    NINA
          If I could only draw like that
          again.

Eddie walks over.

                    EDDIE
          That's what I draw like now.
          Doesn't do me any good.

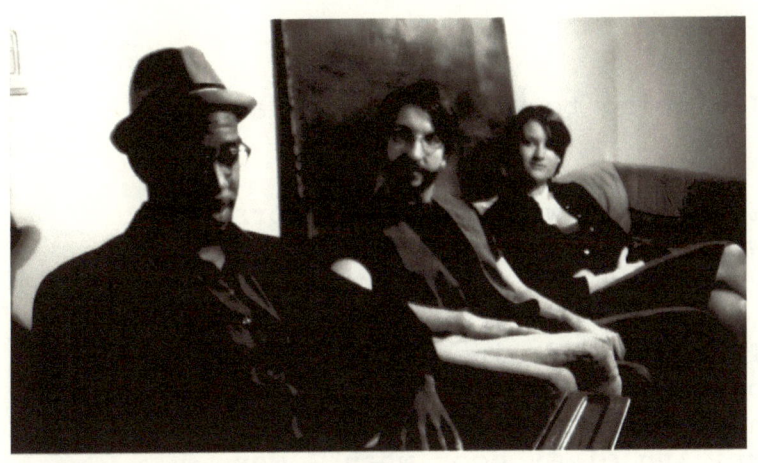

                    NINA
I meant how honest it is. It's
just drawing for the sake of
drawing. Enjoying the smell of
crayons, the big blank paper. You
could just draw and draw for hours
and not think about the end
results. Not the same for my work.

                    EDDIE
Where do you work?

                    NINA
I do freelance graphic design.

                    EDDIE
Why don't you do art for yourself?
In your free time. If I can write
in my free time you can paint in
your free time.

                    NINA
You don't have a job Eddie. All
your time is free time.

                    EDDIE
I'm going to start working again.

                    NINA
You aren't working now? Sorry that
was a trick.

                    EDDIE
I have stuff lined up. You should
be able to do art on your own time
and work. I did most of the
writing of my book when I was
working. You can find time can't
you?

                    NINA
I guess. I just haven't been able
to. So what's this book of yours
about?

                    EDDIE
Oh...it's...uh...about a retired
superhero. He retires but doesn't
know what to do with himself.
Actually it's about a retirement
home for superheroes and-

                    NINA
Eddie-

                    MAX
Heh, Nina. If you could have any
superpower what would you have?

                    NINA
I think superpowers are over-rated.
I'd have an invisible jet.

                    EDDIE
     Interesting.

                    MAX
     I need to use the little boys room.

                    EDDIE
     Me too.

Eddie and Max walk out of the room and down
the hallway.

                    VERONICA
     Did they just go into the bathroom
     together?

                    NINA
     I try to ignore things I don't
     understand about them.

                    VERONICA
     It's great you decided to come out
     with us. Get Eddie's mind off that
     Nina girl. She's all Eddie has
     been talking about tonight.

                    NINA
     Really.

INT. BATHROOM

Eddie and Max walk in.

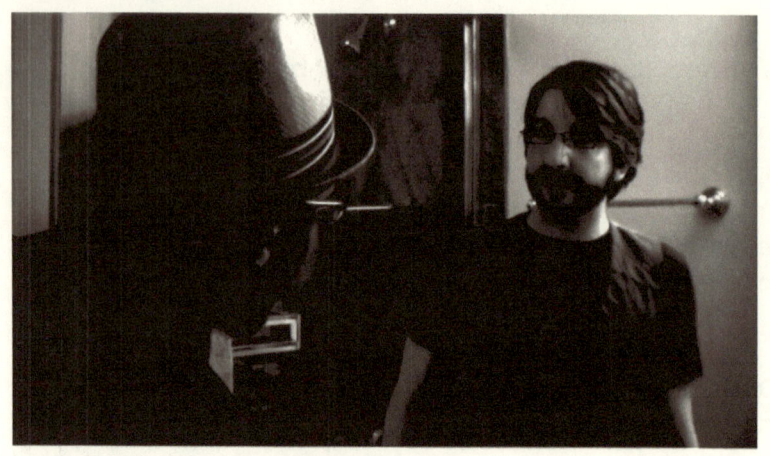

                    EDDIE
          That was close. She would freak
          out if I told her too soon about
          that book. Good call on the
          bathroom thing.

                    MAX
          Eddie I actually have to go to the
          bathroom.

                    EDDIE
          Oh. I should leave.

                    MAX
          Yes. Yes you should. So what is your
          plan?

                    EDDIE
          Plan? I thought you wanted me to
          leave?

                    MAX
I can hold it for a second.

                    EDDIE
I don't have a plan.

                    MAX
You don't have a plan? You want me
to believe that right now you are
just winging it?

                    EDDIE
I have no idea what I am doing
right now.

                    MAX
I know that but you really think
you just want to hang out with her
tonight?

                    EDDIE
Tonight I am just taking things as
they come. I'm not over-thinking things
and I am definitely not planning
anything. I should get back out there.

                    MAX
Yes you should.

                              CUT TO:

Eddie walks in to the living room. Nina sits
on the ground with her arm on the coffee
table over Eddie's book.

Eddie sees it and scrambles to think of

something to say.

                    EDDIE
          I can't believe I was so rude.
          Veronica, Nina, Nina, Veronica.

                    NINA
          Yes Mr. Manners we already did
          that.

                    EDDIE
          Ok. What else were you talking
          about?

                    NINA
          Nothing. Just girl talk.

                    EDDIE
          I don't trust girl talk.

Eddie takes the book from under her arm.
He places the book inside the school desk
then sits on the couch.

                    EDDIE (CONT'D)
          Let me clear some room here.

                    NINA
          So how did you get this desk again?

                    EDDIE
          They were throwing them out.

Max walks back into the room.

                    NINA
          You were just walking by the school
          and they were throwing them out?

Max sits next to Veronica on the couch.

                    MAX
          You talking about Eddie getting
          thrown out of our old school?

                    NINA
          We are now.

                    EDDIE
          No. No we aren't.

                    MAX
          See Eddie used to go there at night-

                    EDDIE
          Max.

                    NINA
          Please continue Max.

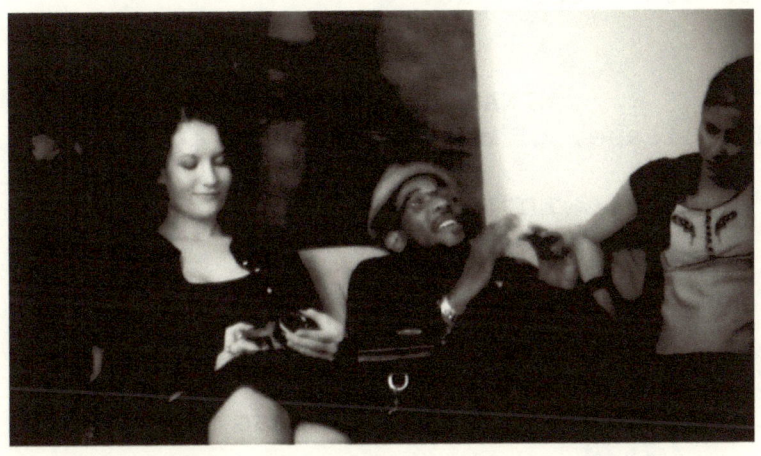

                    MAX
Eddie used to go there at night to
write.

                    NINA
Why?

                    EDDIE
It's free. And I was writing about
my memories of the school. The
janitor used to let me in and I'd
just camp out there.

                    NINA
And then you got kicked out?

                    EDDIE
I know what you're thinking and it
wasn't for bringing a girlfriend
there. I haven't dated anyone
since you. Ok? I know that's what
you are getting at.

                    NINA
No, please. I'm just curious.

                    EDDIE
It's not a great story.

                    MAX
Are you kidding? It's hall of fame.
So Eddie falls asleep and wakes up
in the morning during a class.

                    EDDIE
Obviously, it scared the hell out
of the little kids. I was tucked

away in the corner and somehow no
one had noticed me. Luckily, I was
wearing my old torn coat and looked
vaguely homeless so the teachers
didn't freak out too badly. It was
the middle of the winter and about
twenty below outside, so they just
wrote it off as an act of survival
on my part. In fact they bought me
breakfast and gave me a new coat.
Very nice people.

                NINA
They gave you a new coat?

                EDDIE
Yes.

                NINA
And you took it?

                EDDIE
I was barely making rent then.

                NINA
In your mind, that's close enough
to actually being homeless?

                EDDIE
My coat was pretty ripped. Besides,
I didn't want to get Henry fired.
I was doing it for him.

                NINA
Henry's the janitor?

                EDDIE
Yes.

                    NINA
You're always looking out for
everyone else in this cold, hard
world aren't you?

                    EDDIE
I gave the shoes back.

                    NINA
They gave you shoes too?

                    EDDIE
Yeah. I told you. They're really
nice people.

                    NINA
You gave the shoes back because you felt
guilty? Hopefully.

                    EDDIE
No, they were rubbing in the back.
They were too tight.

                    NINA
You never cease to amaze me Eddie.
No wonder you want to stay up all
night tonight, you probably can't
sleep with some of the things you
have done.

                    EDDIE
You don't have to get mean.

                    NINA
I'm not getting-You know what? Can
you guys excuse us?

Nina gets up and walks into Eddie's bedroom.

                    NINA (CONT'D/O.S)
          Us means you and me Edward.

Eddie slowly gets up and goes into the
bedroom.

                Max
              (To Veronica)
          Told you it was a good story.

                                    CUT TO:

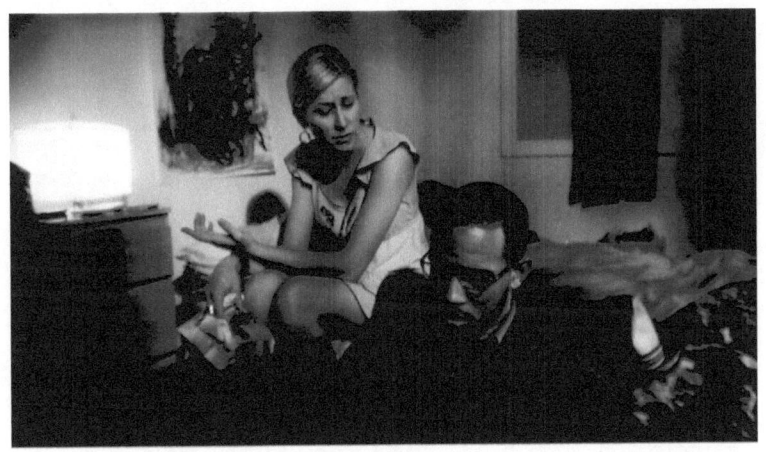

                    NINA
          Have a seat.

                    EDDIE
          Alright.

                    NINA
          I'm not getting mean. You just put
          people in awkward situations with
          your little schemes.

                    EDDIE
I don't have schemes.

                    NINA
Eddie. Something is going on here.
I haven't seen you in a year and
within hours of bumping into you,
I'm wrapped up in another adventure.
I don't know how you do it but you
do it.

                    EDDIE
No one is holding a gun to your head
to be here.

                    NINA
I know.

                    EDDIE
You are in charge of your life, you
can't blame anyone for where you
are in life but you.

                    NINA
I'm not blaming you for being here.
Although I have a feeling that you
blame me for where you are right
now.

                    EDDIE
I'm not blaming you for anything.
Breaking up and the way we broke up
didn't help. It didn't make me a
stronger person. Maybe now it has
after some time but not back then.

                    NINA
It was bad but it wasn't the end of
the earth. The world didn't explode
and catch on fire. You are so
melodramatic.

                    EDDIE
We were together for seven years
and we have known each other since
we were kids. I sort of expected
you to be in my life.

                    NINA
That was the problem Eddie. You
got too comfortable. People break
up all the time and they get over it.

                    EDDIE
You really have moved on.

                    NINA
Are you saying you haven't?

                    EDDIE
No I have. I just don't think
about the break-up in such a
detached way.

                    NINA
I'm not detached. It was bad for
me too Eddie but you have to keep
moving. I'm not going to play it
over and over again in my head.
It's not healthy for you to do that.

                    EDDIE
Don't you remember that day? I had

my glasses in my hands, they got
knocked out when you grabbed my arm
and then that bike ran over them?
I got down trying to find them, I
looked up and all I could see was
your out of focus face. I got up
and you were gone. I couldn't see
anything. It took me hours to get
home. No one would help me. It
took me a week to get new glasses.
I couldn't see. I couldn't do anything.
I got fired. You remember how much
of a jerk my boss was back then.
I spent the whole week lost.

                NINA
I'm sorry Eddie. We just let
things get out of control. I just
had to move on.

                EDDIE
I think about us a lot. In fact,
I wrote a book about us.

                NINA
You did?

                EDDIE
Yes. It's called 'Biting the
Hand.' It's told from the
perspective of our cat. Remember
Charles.

                NINA
Little Charlie. I miss him.

                EDDIE
Remember how he used to sit at that

stool in the kitchen and just watch
us? That's the idea. It's sort of
a tell-all about us. Remember how
we'd be in the living room and he
would jump on the kitchen table and
jump on my typewriter and we joked
that he was actually writing. Well
this is what I think he would write.
He even plays the piano.

                    NINA
We didn't have a piano.

                    EDDIE
We do in the story. Actually that
is what I was working on when I was
going to the school to write. It
follows our whole story together.
All the way back to that school desk.

                    NINA
You are too much Eddie. Can I read
it? I'm afraid to but I think I
want to.

Eddie leaves the bedroom and walks back to
the living room.

Max and Veronica sit on the couch. Max
plays the guitar.

                    EDDIE
Excuse me. Sorry to interrupt.

Eddie reaches into the desk and picks up a
nearly three inch thick block of paper that
is held together by large rubber bands.

Eddie returns to the bedroom and places the monstrosity in front of her.

> NINA
> What is this?

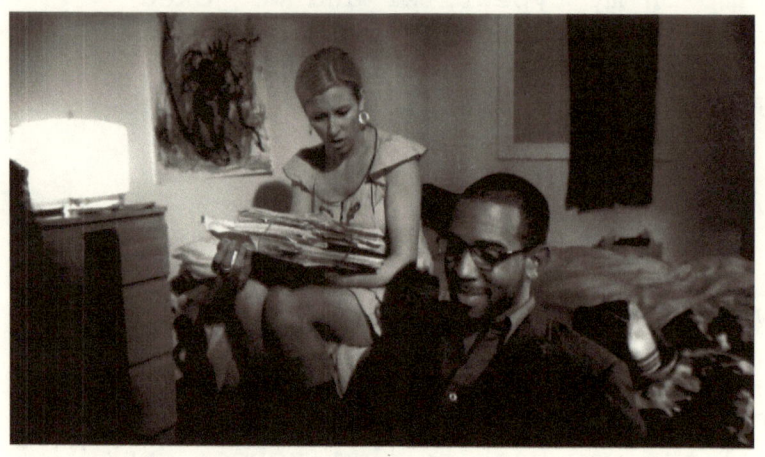

> EDDIE
> This is the book.   It might need some editing.

> NINA
> Do you think?   Is this every conversation we ever had?   How long is it?

> EDDIE
> I don't know exactly but somewhere around twelve hundred pages I think.   Give or take a page.

> NINA
> I don't know what to say.   It's overwhelming.

                    EDDIE
You don't have to read it all in
one night.

                    NINA
No, not the book. You are
overwhelming. What am I supposed
to think about all of this Eddie?
I haven't seen you and then you
show me this. I don't know what
to think.

                    EDDIE
Let's not think about it. Let's
just go with the flow.

                    NINA
Where is the flow going to take
you? It's nice to say you want
to stay up all night and live every
moment but you don't have a job.
I do. I have to get up early Eddie.

                    EDDIE
Why think about it right now?
Let's just enjoy tonight and I'll
figure that all out tomorrow.

                                    CUT TO:

                    MAX
What kind of photos do you like to
take?

                    VERONICA
People in real moments. I don't
like having people pose, so I just
take them whenever. I have my

degree in photography.

                    MAX
Nice.

                    VERONICA
I am trying to get into a gallery
next month. So you should play me a
song now.

                    MAX
I should?

                    VERONICA
Yes. It's the perfect time.

                    MAX
I don't know what to play. I have
been pretty caught up in other
things.

                    VERONICA
It will be good.

Veronica takes the guitar. She plays
horribly.

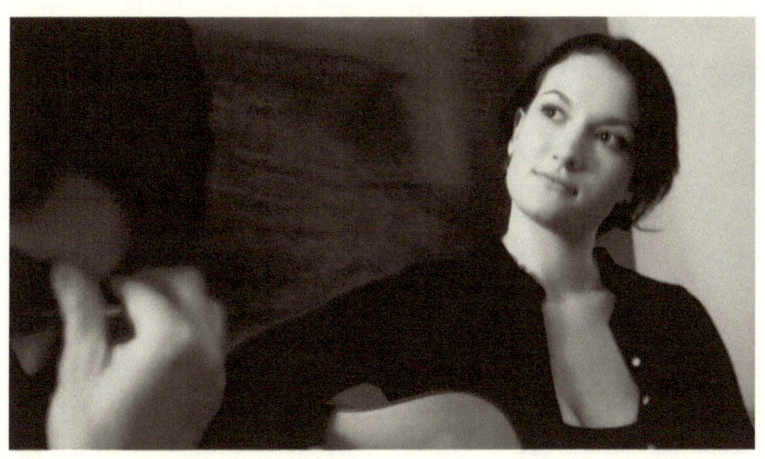

                    MAX
What was that?

                    VERONICA
That was the average person playing
the guitar. Now I know what you
are going to play is going to be
better than that right? If that's
the best I can do I wouldn't worry
about what you are about to play for
me.

Max strums his guitar. It is horribly
out of tune.

                    MAX
Eddie!

                    EDDIE (O.S.)
I didn't play it!

Max tunes the guitar.

                    VERONICA
          What's wrong?

                    MAX
          The guitar is out of tune.

                    VERONICA
          So I'm not as bad as it sounded?

                    MAX
          No you are bad but that didn't
          help.

Veronica takes a picture of him while he is
tuning the guitar.

A large painting leans against the wall.

                    VERONICA
          Who did this painting?

                    MAX
          My dad. He's an artist. An old
          band I was in, we used that for
          an album cover.

                    VERONICA
          What band?

                    MAX
          The Wonderkind.

                    VERONICA
          I know that band. I saw you play
          in New York.

                    MAX
          You did?

                         VERONICA
          Yes. Play me something new. You
          still write don't you?

                           MAX
          Sure. Let me think.

He strums the guitar a few times.

                         VERONICA
          That's ok. Kind of slow.

                           MAX
          No I'm just thinking. Well I do
          have one but it might seem kind of
          depressing or sappy.

                         VERONICA
          That's for me to decide.

Max smiles then plays a song.

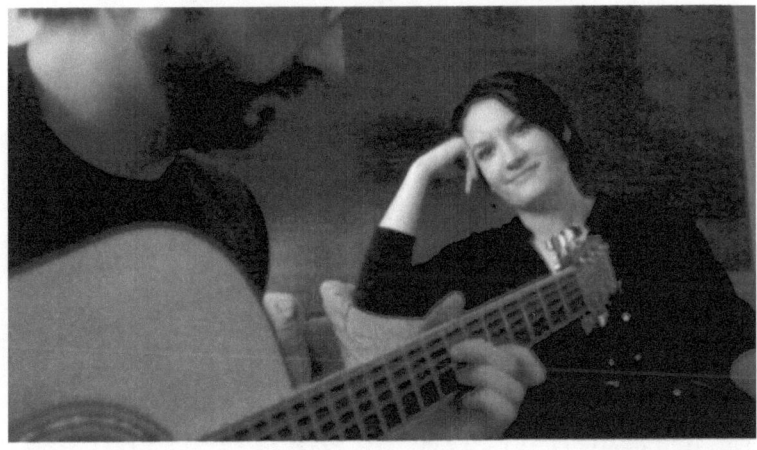

                                        FADE OUT.

INT. EDDIE/MAX APARTMENT-NIGHT-LATER

Eddie, Nina, Max, and Veronica sit on the
floor.

                NINA
      I have to say you do seem more
      relaxed Eddie. You actually do.

                EDDIE
      It's meditation.

                NINA
      You are meditating?

                EDDIE
      Why is that weird?

                NINA
      You can sit quietly for a length of
      time? I'd like to see that happen.

                EDDIE
      Let's do it.

                NINA
      Now?

                VERONICA
      We should all do it here on the
      floor. Oh that sounded weird.

                MAX
      I'm not sure if I'm up for a spirit
      realm adventure with Eddie. I have
      enough of those when we're awake.

                    VERONICA
No it'll be good. We can all get
in tune with each other. You know
certain Indian tribes sleep near
each other and then they meet up in
their dreams and go on adventures
together.

                    EDDIE
Is that like the whole animals and
condiments thing or are you being
serious?

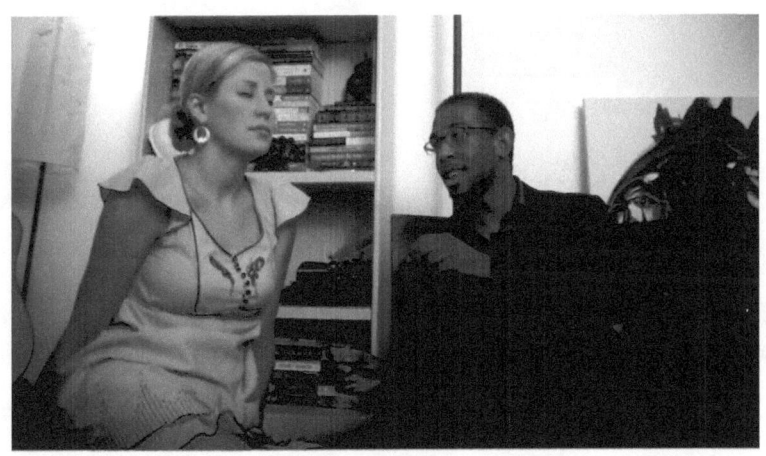

                    VERONICA
I'm completely serious.

                    EDDIE
So let's just breathe deeply and
relax.

The four of them relax and there is nothing

but their breathing as Eddie counts out
loud.

As everyone begins to relax Eddie leans over
and grabs Nina scaring her.

                    EDDIE
          Nina!

                                   FADE OUT

INT. EDDIE/MAX APARTMENT-NIGHT-LATER

There is a knock on the door.

                    EDDIE
          Come on in.

The neighbor enters.

                    NEIGHBOR
          Still inviting danger huh? Oh I'm
          sorry I didn't know you had people
          over.

                    VERONICA
          Hello!

                    NEIGHBOR
          Hello.

Neighbor looks at Nina.

                    NEIGHBOR
          You look really familiar.

                    NINA
Well I'm on t.v. a lot.

                    NEIGHBOR
You are?

                    NINA
No, I'm just kidding.

                    NEIGHBOR
Oh. Eddie can you help me move
something real quick?

                    EDDIE
Sure.

Eddie stands and heads to the door. He
stops and turns around.

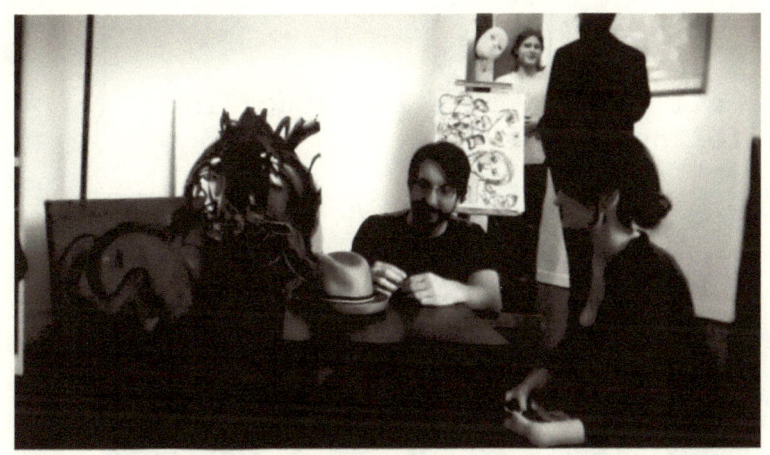

                    EDDIE
                 (to Max)
Now don't let her sweet talk you
into letting her leave.

Eddie leaves.

> MAX
>
> I'm surprised you're still here.
> This would be your time to escape.

> NINA
>
> I can leave any time I want to.

> MAX
>
> Can you?

> NINA
>
> How have you been?

> MAX
>
> I'm ok. Writing new music. Eddie
> and I are working on our book.
> Slowly but surely.

> NINA
>
> We all seem to be a bit stuck in
> life these days.

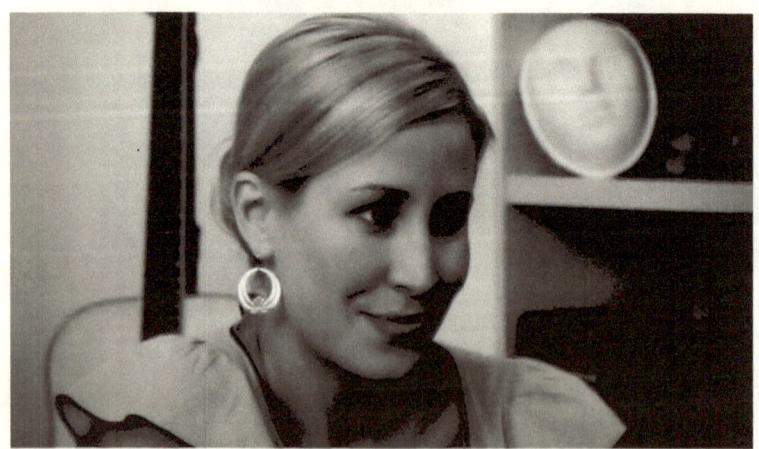

                    MAX
Did I say I was stuck?

                    NINA
No...I meant...I'm not...well
maybe I am.

                    MAX
You know Eddie never stopped
talking about you. I think I
earned a degree in psychology
just talking him out of his
depression. That week he spent
after you...well when you two
broke up. It was a dark time.

                    NINA
You took my place then huh?

                    MAX
Your place?

                    NINA
Max. Eddie was never the same
after he lost his mother. He used
to carry around in his wallet the
one photo of him and his mother.
I used to tell him to put it
somewhere safe so nothing happens
to it but he just wanted her near
him I guess.

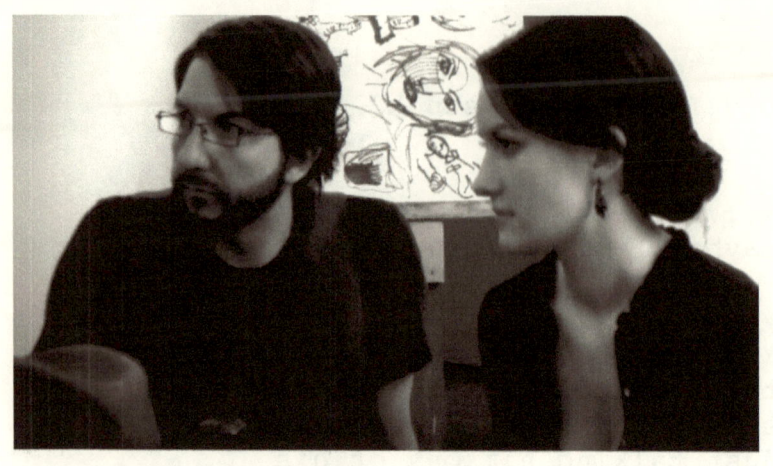

MAX
He still carries it with him.

NINA
He does?

Veronica appears upset.

NINA
(to Veronica)
Are you ok?

VERONICA
It's just sad.

NINA
It is sad. But I couldn't replace her you know. At first it was just subconscious. Taking care of him, trying to keep him moving forward, but after some time I realized I couldn't keep it up.

                    MAX
It can be a full time job.

                    NINA
One was enough for me.

                    MAX
How is your job?

                    NINA
It's...a job. So how did you
two meet?

                    MAX
This is actually our first date.

                    NINA
What?

                    MAX
It is.

                    NINA
And you have been caught in Eddie's
little tractor beam huh? You
should go out and do something.
Actually I should leave. You two
don't need us arguing, that's not
a lot of fun.

                    VERONICA
No it's not a lot of fun but if
you left, you would be by yourself,
then Eddie would be by himself and
it would be depressing.

                    MAX
What should we do?

                    VERONICA
          Anything, let's just go out some-
          where and wander around. I can't
          take anymore pictures of people
          sitting on a couch.

Max, Veronica and Nina stand up.

Eddie returns.

He looks back and forth at Max, Veronica and
Nina.

                    EDDIE
          Were you just talking about me?

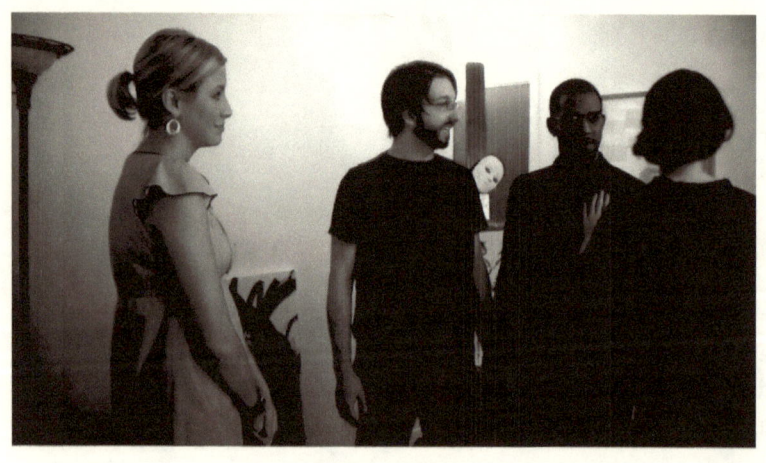

                    VERONICA
          Eddie we are leaving.

                    EDDIE
          Where are we going?

They all walk past him and out the door.

                    EDDIE (cont'd)
        Guys?   Where are we going?

EXT. STREETS-NIGHT

Improvised scenes.

We see Eddie, Nina, Veronica and Max break
into someone's backyard and bounce on their
trampoline.

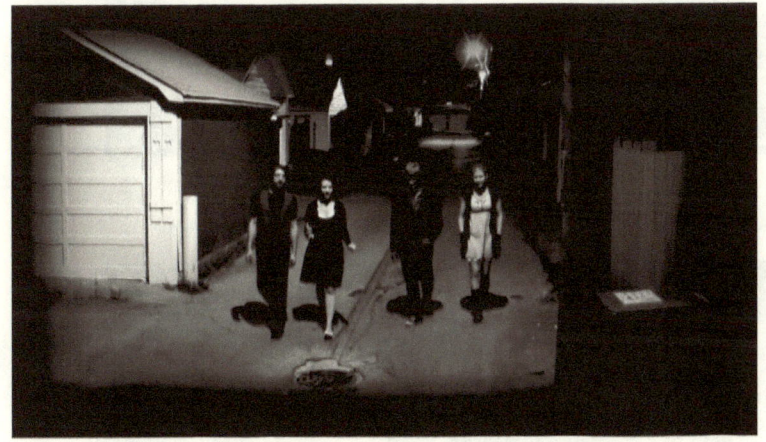

                                        CUT TO:

Eat at a dive Chinese restaurant.   The owner
brings a frisbee with a key to the table.
Max emphatically hands it to Eddie.
Veronica laughs.

                                        CUT TO:

They walk down the street with ice cream.

CUT TO:

They go bowling.

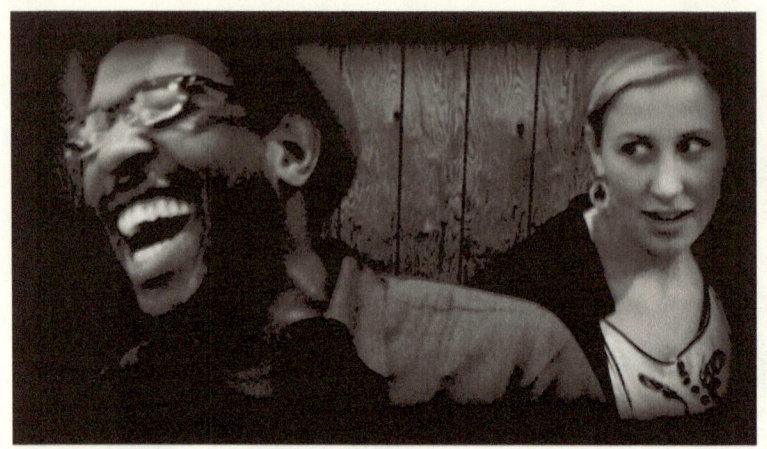

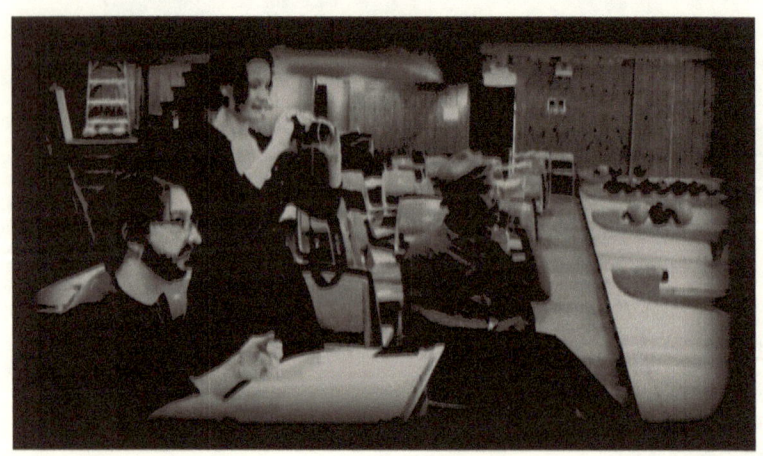

CUT TO:

They sit in a park and admire the stars.

                              CUT TO:

Eddie hides from Veronica's attempt to take
his picture.

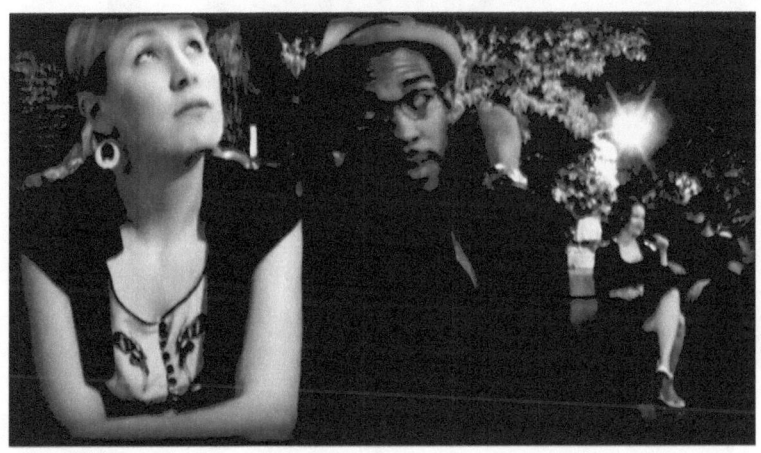

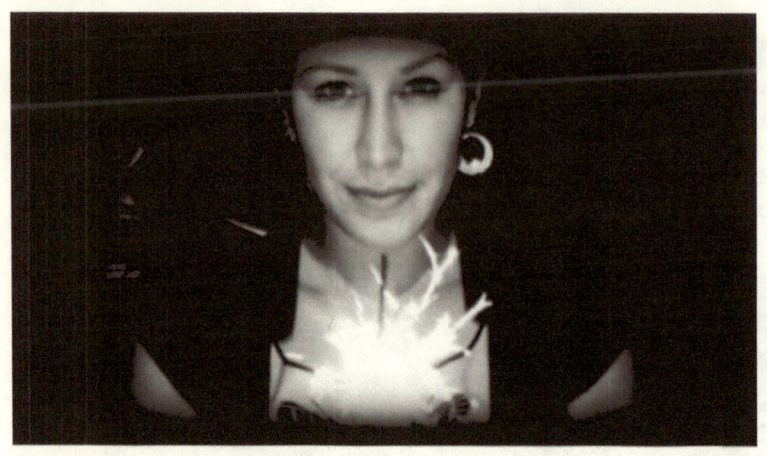

FADE OUT

EXT. ALLEY-NIGHT

Eddie, Max, Nina, and Veronica walk down an
alley.

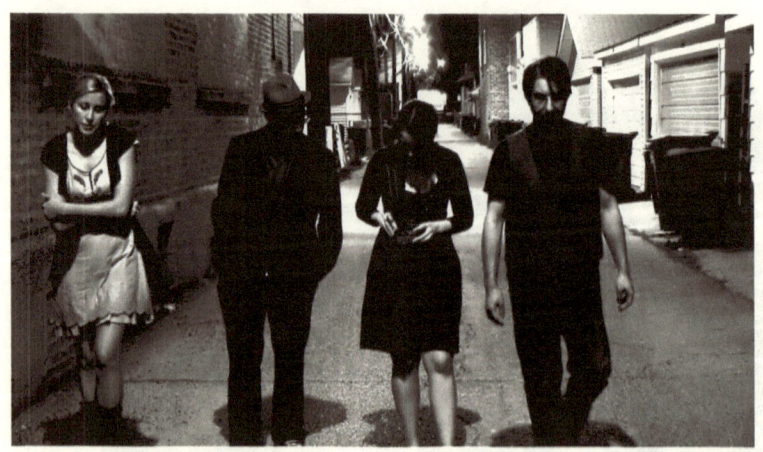

Nina stops and leans against the alley wall.
She takes off her boot.

                    EDDIE
              (to Nina)
          What's wrong?

                    NINA
          These boots weren't exactly made
          for hiking.

                    EDDIE
          You aren't exactly prepared for a
          zombie attack.

                    VERONICA
          I hate zombies.

                    EDDIE
              (points to Veronica)
          She wouldn't last long I can tell
          you that.

                    NINA
          During a zombie attack?

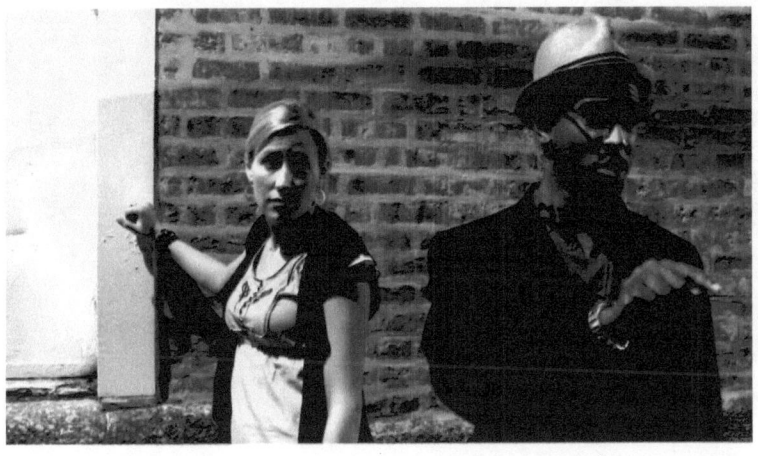

                    EDDIE
Yes. She would just curl up in
fear and lose it. She'd be the
first to go. And then that means
she would become a zombie. Max you
have to come to terms with the fact
that she may not make it.

                    NINA
What are you talking about?

                    EDDIE
Survival. I always have dreams
where I am running around and
trying to stay alive. You see it
in horror movies all the time. I
think overall I would do pretty
well.

                    MAX
How about me?

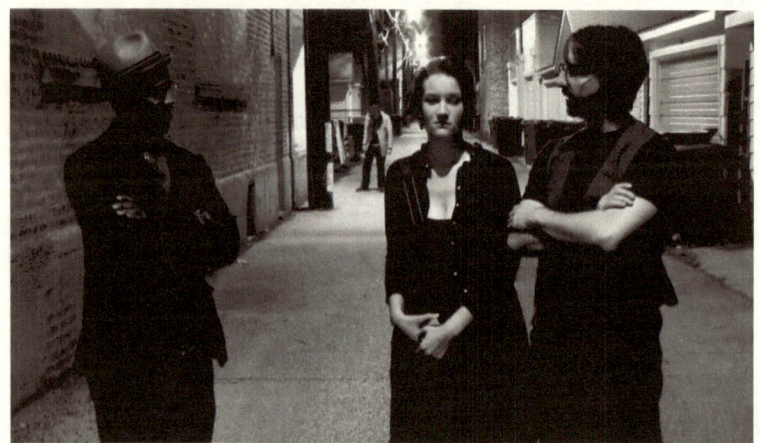

                    EDDIE
Well. You are fairly in shape,
male, smart. How good are you at
running and jumping?

                    MAX
I haven't had to do either
recently, but I bet I could pull
it together if I was being chased
by the undead.

                    EDDIE
You might be the weak link, though.
Clearly she isn't going to make
it since she hates zombies. So
she is going to be one of those
undead chasing you. That might
make you a liability.

                    NINA
You are insane.

                    EDDIE
Why?

                    NINA
Because you are proud of being
prepared in case of a zombie
attack?

                    EDDIE
Yes. And you, quite frankly, are
not.

                    NINA
What do you mean?

                    EDDIE
          Look at your shoes. Totally
          impractical for running.

                    NINA
          I'm wearing these because of work.
          I had to do a presentation today
          and then I went out to that party
          with people from work. It's
          because I have a job Eddie. I may
          not be prepared for a zombie attack
          but you know what I am prepared
          for? Paying rent.

                    EDDIE
          All I am saying is-

A loud moan echoes through the alley.

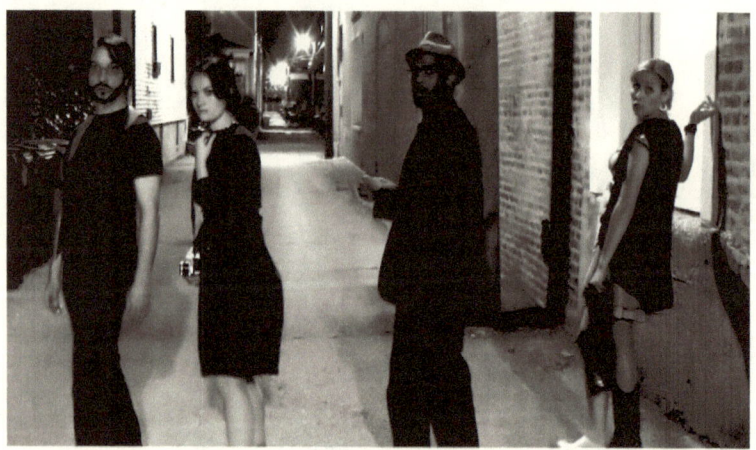

They all freeze.

Another moan echoes through the alley.

They all turn around slowly.

A man in tattered clothes slowly staggers in the alley.

                    EDDIE
          I told you.

                    NINA
          That's a bum.

                    EDDIE
          Yeah, a Zombie bum.

Veronica runs off first then the others follow.

EXT. PARK-NIGHT

Eddie and Max walk in to a park. Nina and Veronica trail behind them.

                    MAX
          I wish you would have told me
          about not paying the rent.

                    EDDIE
          It's no big deal. We can take this
          money and make something happen for
          us. And if you don't want to do it
          then I'll give your money back and we
          can just move someplace else. This
          money is going to get us where we
          need to go.

Eddie taps his wallet.

                    MAX
        You have the money with you?

                    EDDIE
        Yeah, I wasn't going to leave it
        laying around the apartment.

                    MAX
        Maybe you should give it to me.

Veronica and Nina catch up.

                    VERONICA
        Max I want to take your picture
        over there.

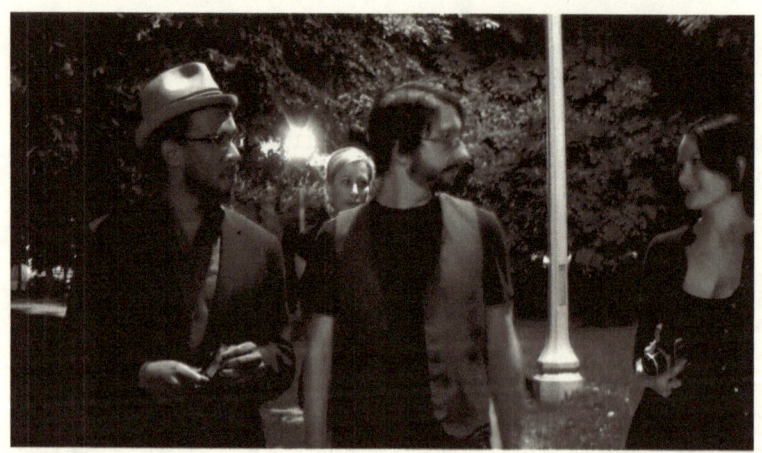

Veronica walks away.   Max follows.

Nina walks past Eddie and into the open
field. He follows.

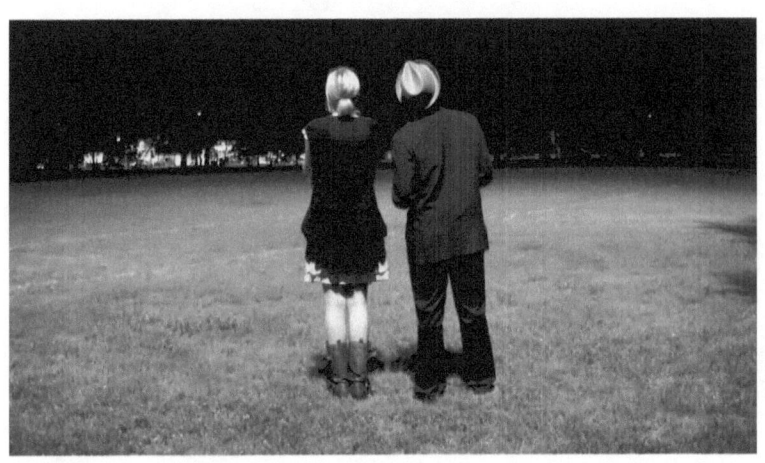

                    EDDIE
                 (to Nina)
If you could get in a space ship
and just fly out into space, would
you do it?

                    NINA
Just go for a ride? Sure.

                    EDDIE
No. You would be some test subject.
You could just drift into space for
as long as you can live. You could
see things no one would ever see.
You have to die sometime right?
Imagine all the things you could see.

                    NINA
You have way too much time on your
hands Eddie.

                    EDDIE
Life is full of choices. You are
the sum total of all your choices.

So when you answer a question like
that it tells what kind of person
you are.

            NINA
Am I interviewing for a job?
I still think you have too much
time on your hands. Someone needs
to save you from your nihilistic
perspectives Eddie. You know that?
You are always trying to get away
from this planet.

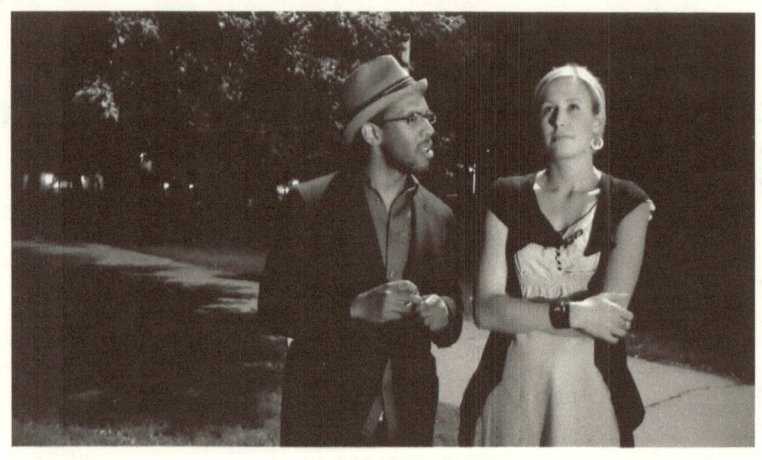

            EDDIE
I'm not a nihilist. I just believe
there is lots of stuff out there.

            NINA
There is a lot of stuff on Earth
too but you don't seem to be all
that interested in it. Why don't
you spend more time here with the
rest of us?

                    EDDIE
You're like this beautiful little
cloud that just never runs out of
rain.

EXT. PARK-NIGHT

Eddie and Nina sit.

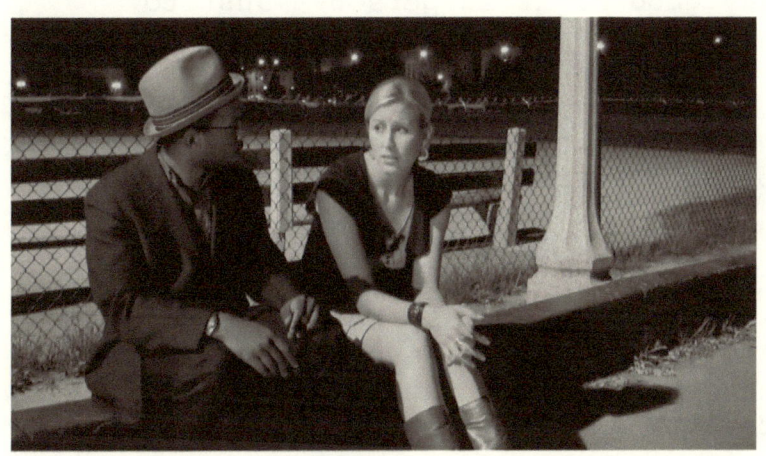

                    EDDIE
I guess we should start heading
downtown to the observatory.

                    NINA
Eddie, I have to get to bed.
I work in a few hours.

                    EDDIE
One night is not going to kill you.
Besides you promised.

                    NINA
Don't be a child. Don't ruin

tonight. We can go out some other
time.

                    EDDIE
That's not good enough. People
always say that but they don't mean
it. Don't you remember the first
summer we were together I used to
drive an hour to see you just to
say good night in person. Just to
give you a good night kiss.

                    NINA
What does that have to do with me
being a wreck tomorrow at work?

                    EDDIE
Everything. If you want to live
life then we have to do it now not
some other time. We are going to
head to the observatory and wait
for the sunrise.

                    NINA
You know if you are serious about
trying to be part of my life and
for us to start over again, it
would be nice if you had both a
place to live and a job. Like a
normal person.

                    EDDIE
A normal person?

                    NINA
I understand what you and Max are
trying to do but eventually you
have to move on and grow up.

                    EDDIE
I don't want to lose who I am
just to become a grown up.
Whatever that means. I like me.

                    NINA
I like you too. But since the last
time we saw each other you haven't
really moved forward very much have
you? Eddie. When are you going to
take charge of your life? When?
Are you blaming me for where you
are in life? Because if you are
then there is no hope for us to
even be friends. Let alone
whatever else is cooking up in that
brain of yours.

                    EDDIE
I'm not blaming you. It's just...I
don't even know how to say it.

                    NINA
If you can't let go of the past
Eddie there's no hope for a future.
Not for yourself, let alone for us.

                    EDDIE
You have to admit that you are part
of why I am stuck, it's not like
you had nothing to do with it.

                    NINA
     (breathes deeply)
You haven't changed Eddie. Part of
me believes you never are going to
either.

                    EDDIE
Why would you say that?

                    NINA
You want so much from me but you
don't demand the same from yourself.
If you decide to grow up then maybe
we can hang out. But until then I
think we need to just be apart.

Max and Veronica catch up.

                    MAX
So what's the plan?

                    NINA
I'm heading home Max. It was nice
to meet to you Veronica.

                    EDDIE
She's not heading home.

                    VERONICA
If she is tired then we can do this
again some other time.

                    EDDIE
              (to Veronica)
No offense, you're a nice girl but
this is none of your business.

                    MAX
Don't talk to her like that Eddie.

                    EDDIE
Why is she getting involved?

                    NINA
          Goodbye.

                    EDDIE
          Nina.

                    MAX
          Eddie. You can't do this. We are
          heading home to pack. We're
          packing because of you right now.
          Just let it go.

                    NINA
          Packing for what?

                    MAX
          Our fearless leader got us
          kicked out of our apartment.

                    EDDIE
          I didn't get us kicked out.

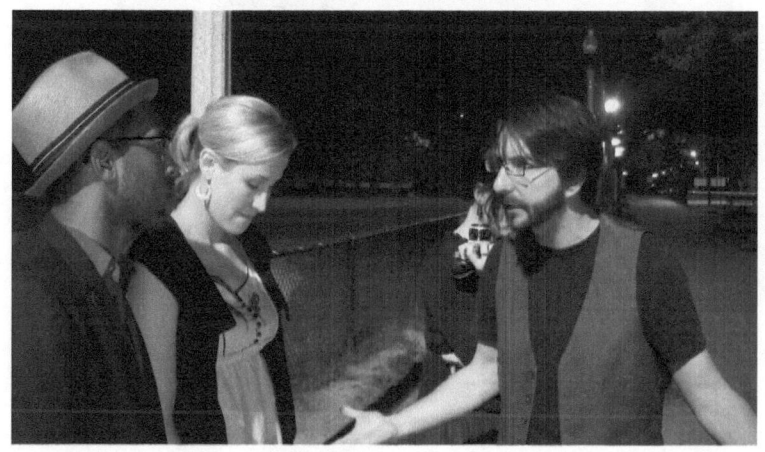

                    MAX
          Even if you hadn't been stashing

the rent money away it would have
been nice to know we were getting
kicked out. So, you know, I could
find a new place to live.

                    NINA
This is too much for me. Eddie, I
have to go.

Eddie stands as Nina, Max and Veronica walk
away in opposite directions. He doesn't
know which way to go.

EXT. STREET-NIGHT

Nina walks slowly home.

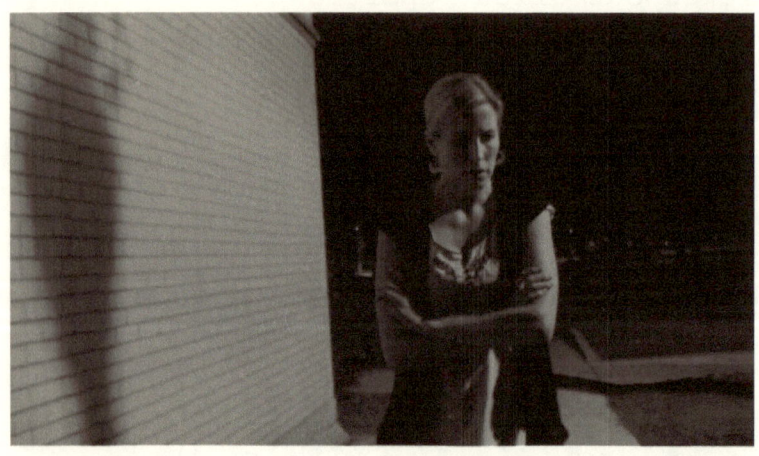

INT. NINA'S APARTMENT-NIGHT

Nina walks in and stands in her apartment.
She is lost in thought.

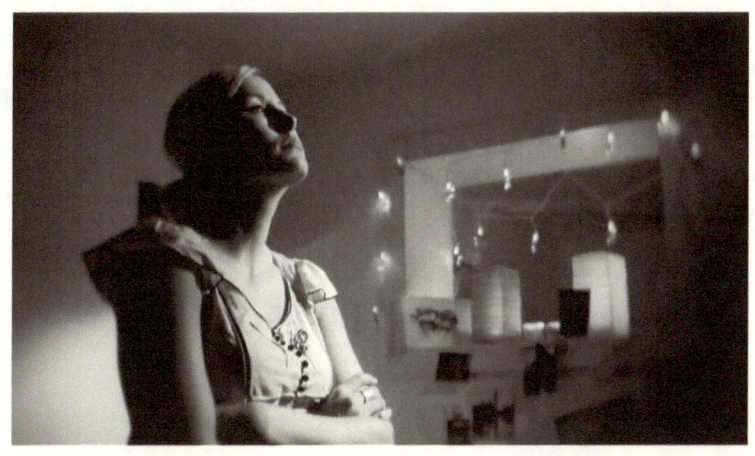

Nina sees a piece of paper on the ground.

She picks it up and places it back on the
wall next to an old photo of Eddie and her.

She takes the photo off the wall and reads
the poem written on it.

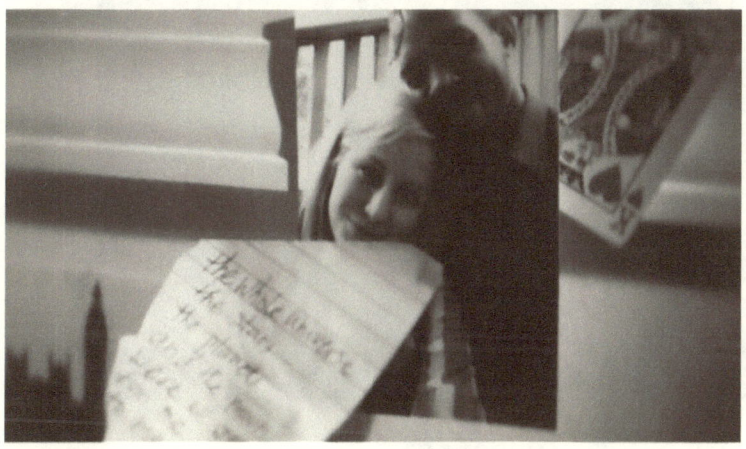

It reads:

"The whole universe,
the stars, the planets and the moon
were all created for me to meet you.
Love...Eddie"

EXT. VERONICA'S APARTMENT-NIGHT

        MAX
I'm sorry that this night ended the
way it did but I had a great time.

        VERONICA
So did I.

        MAX
You did?

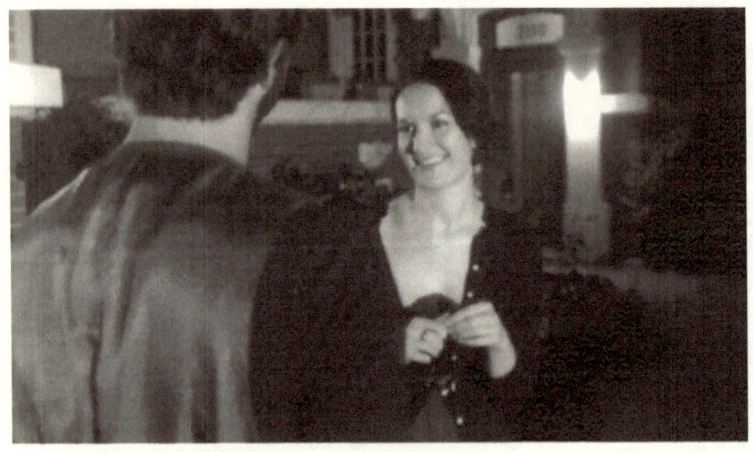

        VERONICA
Yes. Eddie's so wrapped up in his
own little world and seeing Nina
for the first time. He doesn't

even know what he was saying.

                    MAX
He should. But anyway. I'm going
to catch a cab.

                    VERONICA
We should do this again.

                    MAX
We should.

Veronica begins to walk up the stairs. She
stops and comes back to Max.

                    VERONICA
You know there are actually two
things that separate humans from
animals.

                    MAX
Really? It's more complicated than
just the use of condiments?

                    VERONICA
Yes. People get nervous and say
things that they think the other
person wants to hear. When really
the other person just wants to hear
the truth. I don't think animals
do that.

                    MAX
No I don't think they do. Of
course I don't think animals go on
a lot of blind dates. If they did I
bet they would want to put their best
foot or paw forward.

                    VERONICA
                (breathing deeply)
I have no idea what I'm doing with
myself. I have a college degree in
something I'm terrible at. And
even if I *was* good at it, what
would I even do with it? All those
things I said about myself are
things I want to be not things I
really am.

                    MAX
You didn't have to get nervous.
Who am I to get nervous about?

                    VERONICA
You're a great guy that's who you
are. I figured if you didn't like
me you would have just run away.
That was why I guess Eddie was
there, but you turned out to be
really sweet. I thought if you
didn't like me you would never find
out about me but I want you to know
all about me. That sounded weird.

                    MAX
                (laughs)
No I know what you mean. But you
shouldn't be so worried about
yourself. No one knows what they
are doing with themselves. For
example, me. Trust me you have
plenty of time to figure it all
out.

                    VERONICA
The whole point of tonight was
about how short life is. That's
all Eddie has been talking about.

                    MAX
You're listening to Eddie now for
life advice?

                    VERONICA
Not about everything.

                    MAX
Especially after how he talked to
you.

                    VERONICA
I understand why he is how he is.
I understand losing a parent way,
way too soon. I'm not saying he
can do whatever he wants but
everyone deals with things
differently.

                    MAX
You're good at understanding
people.

                    VERONICA
I understand how you feel about me.

                    MAX
You do?

                    VERONICA
Well Eddie used your code word ten
seconds after meeting you and here
we are hours later still together.

                    MAX
Oh.

                    VERONICA
You need a better code word than
timpani.

                    MAX
I don't plan on needing one any time
soon.

EXT. STREETS-NIGHT

Eddie wanders home. He passes a street
drummer.

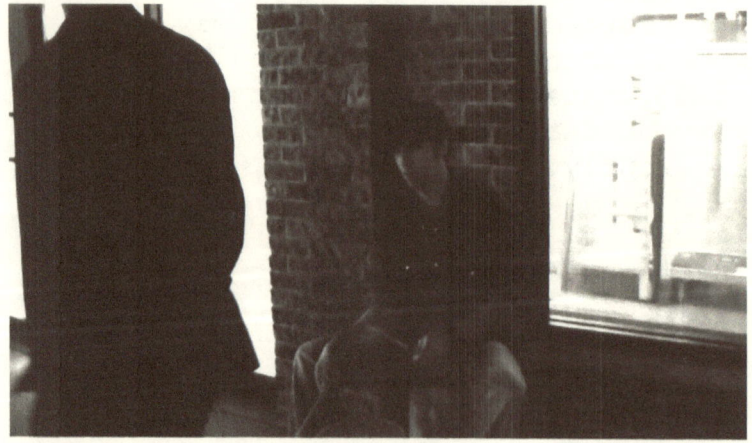

Eddie walks down the sidewalk and is
confronted by two muggers.

One of the guys grabs Eddie's arm.

Another grabs his wallet chain, unhooks it

and takes his wallet. He tosses it to the
main thug.

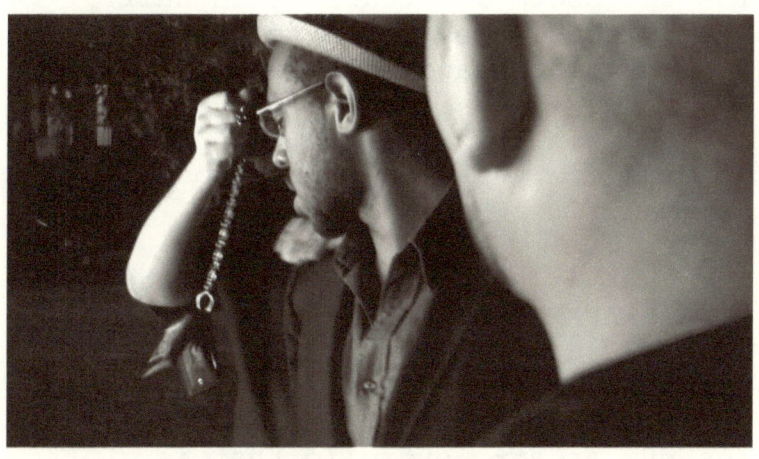

                    EDDIE
        You can have the money in there,
        just give me the picture. You
        don't need a picture of me.

The thug opens the wallet, pulls out the
photo. He tosses the wallet to another guy.

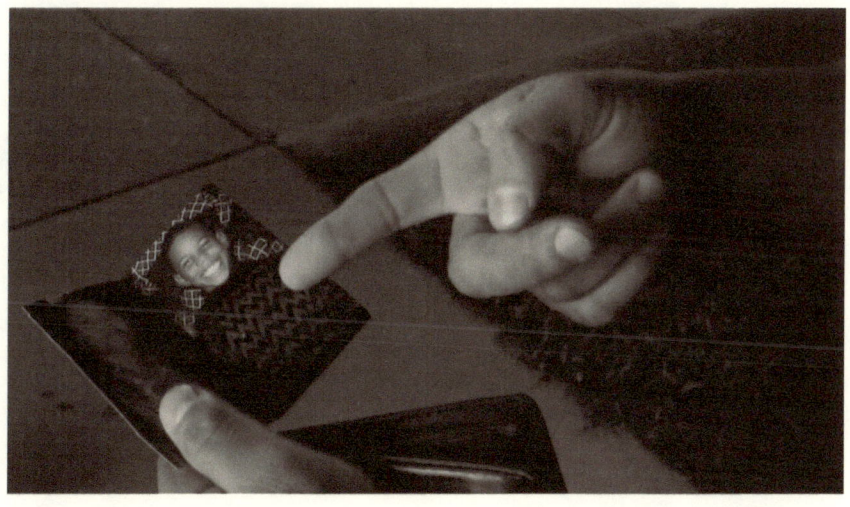

He holds the photo and tears it in half.
Drops the pieces, they float to the
ground. They laugh and walk away.

                    EDDIE (CONT'D)
        You didn't...you didn't have to do
        that man.

INT. NINA'S APARTMENT-NIGHT

Nina opens her closet door.

She digs out an art portfolio that is
buried.

She opens it and pulls out drawings and
paintings.

She finds an old drawing of Eddie. She
stares at the picture for a few moments.

She looks back at the poem on the wall.

She stands, grabs her coat and leaves her
apartment.

                    FADE OUT.

INT. EDDIE'S APARTMENT-NIGHT

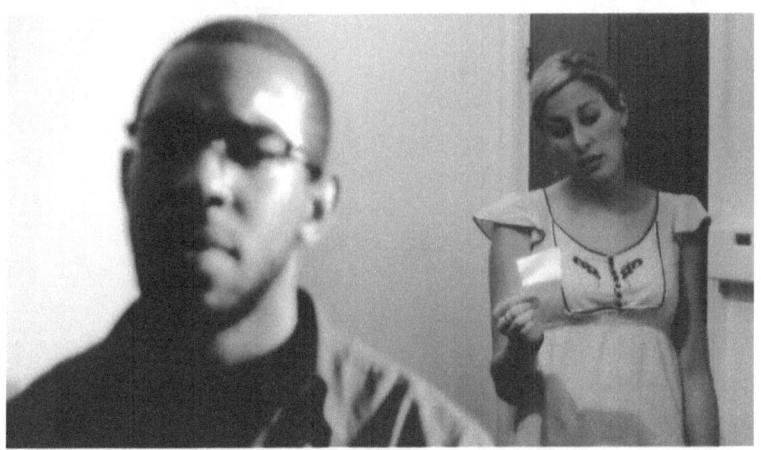

Eddie sits on the ground.

A knock at the door.

                    EDDIE
          Come in.

The door opens, Nina walks in a few steps.

He stands up and turns away from her by the
window.

                    NINA
          The whole universe was created for
          me to meet you. Did you mean that?

                    EDDIE
          Of course.

                    NINA
          If you did mean it then you have to
          do alot more than just write it

down on a piece of paper and give
it to me.

                EDDIE
What can I do?

                NINA
Eddie. Just because I am standing
here right now doesn't mean I have
been sitting around waiting for you
to show up again in my life. It
doesn't mean I am going to follow
you around every time you think of
some crazy adventure like tonight.
I have my own life now and you have
to respect that. But most
importantly, it doesn't mean we are
getting back together again. What
it means is...I miss you. But more
than that...I miss you being in my
life. I had hoped if we ever saw each
other again you would have become a
successful writer or whatever you
wanted to do with yourself. But
instead you don't have a place to
live and the only writing you have
done after all this time is a
ridiculously long book about us,
which honestly is a little scary.

                EDDIE
It wasn't supposed to freak you
out. It wasn't supposed to be so
long either. But once I start
writing about you and how much you
mean to me, I just can't stop. I'm
sorry if it made you uncomfortable.

                    NINA
          I'd still like to read it but I'd
          rather spend time writing a new
          chapter in our story then reliving
          stuff from the past.

                    EDDIE
          I do too.

                    NINA
          Why won't you look at me?

          Eddie turns around. He has a bandaid on
          this head. He has an ice pack in his hand.

                    NINA
          What happened to you?

                    EDDIE
          It's nothing.

          Nina walks over to him.

                    EDDIE
          I can take care of myself.

                    NINA
          No Eddie, you can't! Look where
          taking care of yourself has gotten
          you. Seriously. I don't want to
          even think about if something bad
          had happened to you before we saw
          each other tonight.

          Eddie sits down. She sits down next to him.

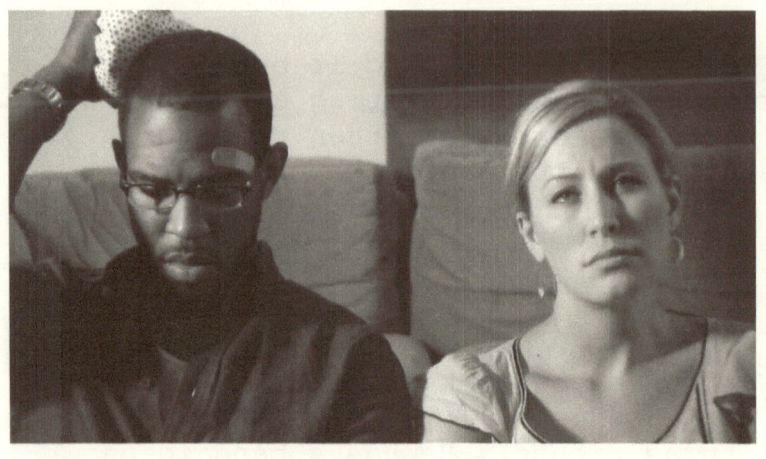

                    NINA (CONT'D)
What am I going to do with you?
How are you going to take care of
yourself? You don't even have a
place to live let alone a job.

                    EDDIE
I have a job.

                    NINA
What are you talking about? If we
are supposed to be starting over
again, lying isn't a good start.

                    EDDIE
I don't have it *yet*. I got offered
a job yesterday. I just have to
call them today and accept it.

                    NINA
When were you going to tell me all
this?

EDDIE

I didn't think I was going to see
you tonight. And then after you
left I didn't think we were ever
going to see each other again. It
just didn't come up. It's a
terrible job so I just kept putting
it out of my mind.

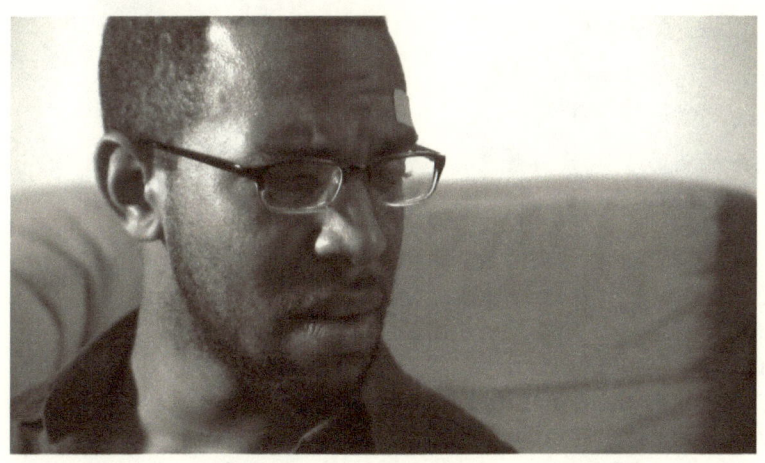

NINA

Well it's time you started facing
things. In reality.

EDDIE

I know, I know. My head is always
in the clouds, I daydream too much,
I don't take anything seriously.

NINA

Those are the things I like about
you. But you have to take charge
of your life. Your book is a great
idea but it's too long. You're
just so scattered right now.

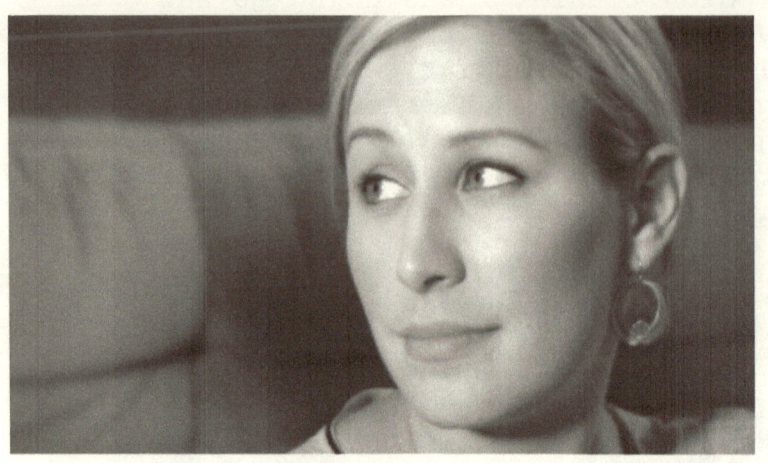

EDDIE
I didn't think you were even going
to talk to me let alone agree to
hang out tonight. I'm lost Nina.
I don't know anything about the
world but I do know that I want you
in my life. And the book kept
getting longer and longer because I
didn't have anything new to say.
Nothing inspires me more than you
so I just kept writing. Nothing
was worth talking about in my life
right now. But after tonight, I
have a lot to say. I don't know
how I'm going to say it all with
nothing.

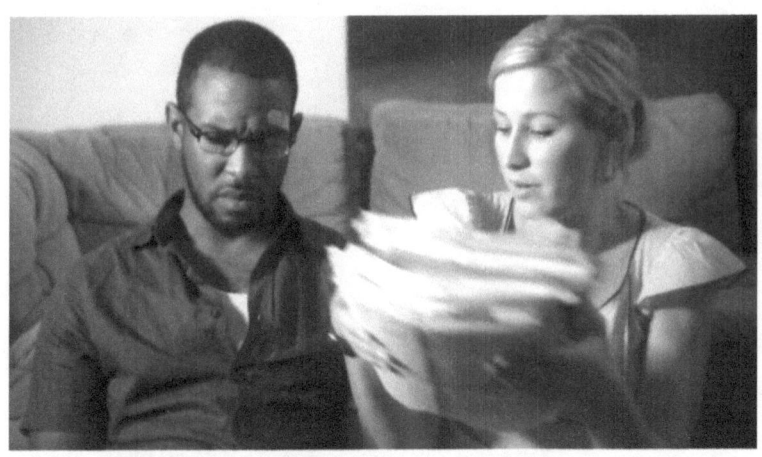

                    NINA
How about twelve-hundred blank
pages?

Nina takes the rubber-banded pages from the
table and flips them around.

She slaps the top of the stack.

                    NINA (CONT'D)
If you have something to say. Then
say it. Don't think about something
you don't have or some dumb job you
have to work. Just write. I'll even
loan you a pen. You have been carrying
around the past way more than most
people do. It's time to let it go.
Because I don't know where I am going
in life either and I don't know anything
about where the world is headed but
I do know you can't hold on to the
past and me at the same time.

Eddie drops the heavy block of paper to the
ground.

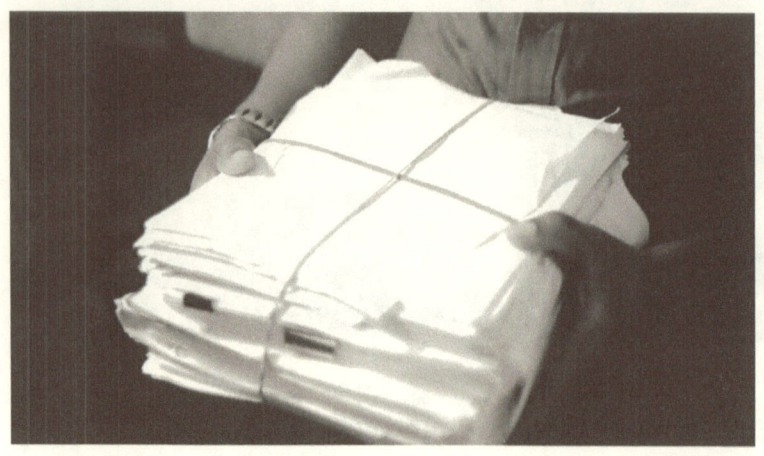

                    NINA (CONT'D)
        I came all the way over here to
        watch the sunset and I don't think
        we can see it from here.

EXT. ROOFTOP-DAYBREAK

He stands and looks across the skyline of
Chicago.

Nina stands next to him, she puts her head
on his shoulder.

                    MAX (O.S.)
        Now this is worth taking a picture of.

Eddie and Nina turn around.

Max and Veronica walk up.

Eddie and Max both nod in silent agreement
that everything is alright between them.

Eddie turns to Veronica.

                    EDDIE
          I didn't mean to talk to you like
          that before.

                    VERONICA
          It's ok. I understand. This wasn't
          exactly a normal night. Next time
          we all hang out I expect a complete
          gentleman.

                    EDDIE
          Next time?

He turns to Nina.

She nods.

                    EDDIE (CONT'D)
          Here take our picture. Can you?

Eddie puts his arm around Nina.

Veronica holds her camera up and clicks the
button but nothing happens.

                    VERONICA
                  (laughs)
          I'm out of film.

Eddie can't believe it. He throws his arms
in the air, turns around in frustration.

He looks across the city at the sun.

                    MAX
We made it.

                    EDDIE
Barely.

                    NINA
Barely is good enough these days.

Eddie, Nina, Max and Veronica stand side by
side in silence as the sunlight begins to
hit their faces.

Eddie turns to Nina.

Nina reaches over and takes Eddie's hand.

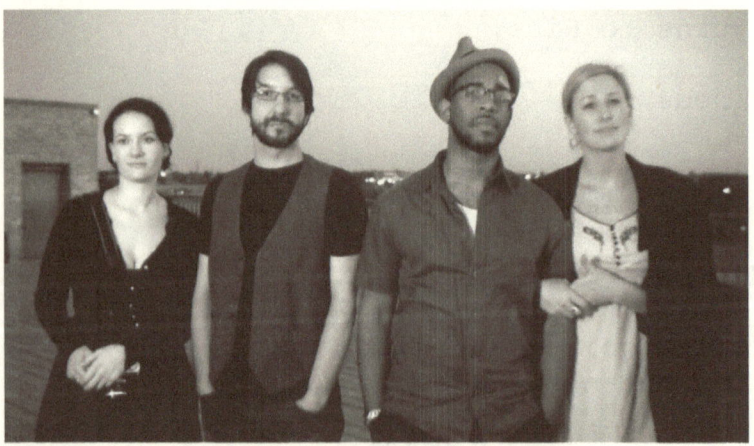

We turn slowly until away from them as we
reach the sun rising over Chicago.

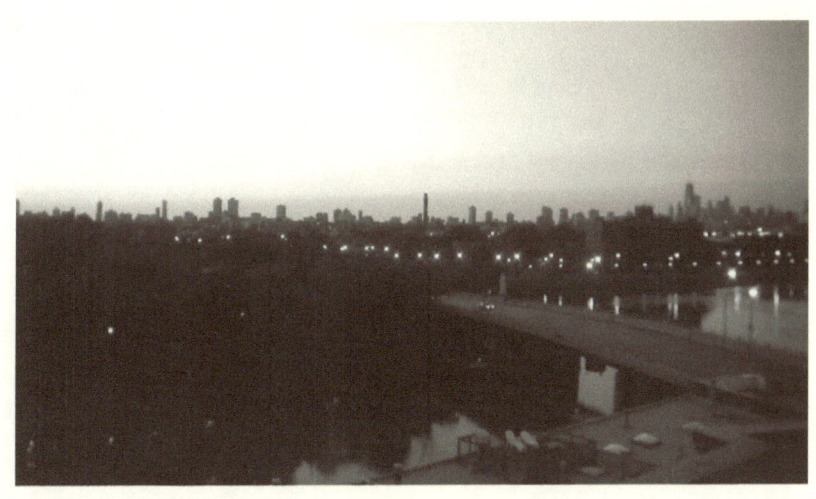

FADE OUT

THE END

EQUIPMENT LIST

CAMERA:

Canon HV30 (24p, shutter priority setting)
Letus Mini DOF Adaptor
Marshall V-LCD70P monitor
Nikon 14mm
Nikon 24mm f2
Nikon 50mm f1.8
Small Tungsten light package: 1000W, 500W
Ladder dolly

SOUND:

702r portable sound device
Schoeps CMC-MK (main boom microphone)
Azden SGM-1X (secondary microphone)
Zoom H4N recorder

EDITING:

MacPro Tower Quadcore 2.66 GHz
(2) 24" LG Monitors
Final Cut Pro 7
Neatvideo plug-in
SoundSoap (audio cleaning program by BIAS)
Magic Bullet: Looks plug-in

REFERENCE GUIDE

http://en.wikipedia.org/wiki/Screenwriting

http://www.creativescreenwriting.com/index.html

http://www.dmoz.org/Arts/Writers_Resources/Screenwriting/

http://www.filmmaking.net/

http://www.indietalk.com/

http://www.imdb.com/indie/

http://www.createspace.com

http://www.indiegogo.com

Rebel Without a Crew by Robert Rodriguez, Plume Publishing, 1996

The Pocket Lawyer for Filmmakers: A Legal Toolkit for Independent Producers by Thomas A. Crowell, Focal Press , 2007

Independent Feature Film Production: A Complete Guide from Concept Through Distribution by Gregory Goodell, St. Martin's Griffin; Revised Edition, 1998

So You Want to be a Producer by Lawrence Turman, Three Rivers Press, 2005

Essentials of Screenwriting by Richard Walter, Plume (Penguin Group), 2010

The Anatomy of Story by John Truby, Faber and Faber, 2007

Final Cut Pro 7 by Rick Young, Focal Press, 2010.

Think Outside the Box Office by Jon Reiss, Hybrid Cinema Publishing, 2010

Stand Out Shorts by Russell Evans, Focal Press, 2010

The Independent Filmmaker's Law and Business Guide by Jon M. Garon Chicago Review Press, 2009.

The Shut Up and Shoot Documentary Guide by Anthony Q. Artis, Focal Press, 2008

Digital Video Production Cookbook by Chris Kenworthy, O'Reilly Media, 2006

The Guerilla Filmmakers Handbook by Genevieve Jollifee and Chris Jones, Continuum, 2004

Master Shots by Chris Kenworthy, Michael Weise Productions, 2009

D.I.Y. (Design it Yourself) edited by Elle Lupton Princeton Architectural Press, 2006

Five Essential Steps in Digital Video by Denise Ohio, Que Corporation, 2002

Cinematography: Theory and Practice by Blain Brown, Focal Press, 2002

Save The Cat! by Blake Snyder, Michael Wiese Productions, 2005

The following excerpt is the prologue from Sebastian J. Howley's novel *Lost and Found in Los Angeles*.

From the back cover:

Killing time in a dead-end cubicle job, a Chicago writer gets a phone call that turns his life upside down. An old friend from college insists that he quit his job and move to Los Angeles to follow his dreams. In the face of a meaningless promotion and a complicated family situation, he makes the leap and begins his journey.

Lost and Found in Los Angeles is a tale of the dark, treacherous land of Hollywood. It is a funny, hopeful and sometimes heartbreaking story. Imaginary monsters, earthquakes, and a movie memorabilia-collecting wizard all shape the journey of a writer who learns that it is never too late to change your life and embrace what is truly important.

It is available in paperback at www.tinyurl.com/lostinla

It is also available for the Kindle.

lost and found in los angeles

a novel

sebastian j. howley

Prologue

Los Angeles isn't a city; it's just a bunch of streets.

At least that's all I could tell during my first few hours there. I was stuck in the web of cars that were sitting, crashing and flying all around me. They don't roll out the red carpet for new comers here. In fact, it felt more like I had extended my hand to meet someone for the first time only to be stared at with crossed-arm indifference. Everyone knows why you are there and no one wants the burden of another transplant. The roads are full of them. If this road was the throat of the city, it would be grasping its neck and breathing its last breath. Somehow, though, it lives on.

I thought I would never make it to my new apartment. I was exhausted from traveling and my nerves were frayed and corrupted by the lack of sleep. All of this magnified the frantic nature of my surroundings. Every road was full of cars. If I had any brains at all, I would have quit writing and opened a gas station. If I had, of course, I'd be changing your oil right now and you wouldn't be reading this book.

Scott and I sped through traffic. We passed three accidents in the course of twenty minutes. I suspect the plastic surgery epidemic is not from vanity after all, but actually from all the routine car accidents. It's funny that a city built on fantasy and escapism is connected by roads that make you feel as if you were always about to die. That was my first realization: I could die before I even got to my new temporary home. In fact, we almost did. That's not how Scott remembers it, but that's how I know it was.

It happened moments after I saw the Hollywood sign for the first time. Scott had picked me up at the train station because I don't fly. We can talk about flying and almost dying later; right now, I want to talk about driving and almost dying. I stepped off the train and noticed the heat immediately. I noticed it in New Mexico and Arizona, but I was just passing through those places; this was my destination. I felt like a piece of bacon dropped onto a frying pan. My face was red and warm. Normally I don't sweat but I was instantly after stepping off the train. It was partially from the heat but mainly from Scott's driving. I had forgotten that he drives as if the world was cracking apart behind him.

I was tired and hungry, dreaming of a shower while the road whipped by. All of a sudden, the forward progress stopped and we sat idling on a three-lane parking lot for what felt like an hour. Impatient and exhausted, I leaned my head against the window. That's when I saw it resting upon its throne on the horizon: the Hollywood sign. It's just a sign I told myself, that is all it is. But it is much more than a sign. You know that and so do I. It is the siren calling fresh blood to its feet. It is an altar we worship at without questioning who runs the church. I am embarrassed to say it, but my eyes welled up. One tear found its way out and down my cheek. I have no idea why. Scott didn't notice, he was yelling at a stretch limo.

We started moving again and I felt stupid almost immediately. How could a sign, just a bunch of letters, make me cry? It was all those dreams I had and mine was there with all the others. I saw my little dream cloud mixing and moving through the sky around the sign, it was all so clear. Everything seemed so simple.

Then Scott slammed on the brakes, we skidded and swerved and slid. We spun around and ended up facing the traffic we were just flowing with. Two cars next to us collided, violently flipping one on its side. Scott hit the gas and turned around quickly on to the median as dirt kicked up and floated all around us.

It became immediately clear what had just happened.
We almost just died.

Scott looked at me.
"Don't worry. This happens all the time."
We sat there stuck. The lone tear was still on my cheek.
Scott shook his head.
"Don't be such a baby, there's no reason to be crying, we're fine."
I ignored him and looked out the window.
I couldn't see the Hollywood sign anymore and the daydream was over.

The cars sped by us. I felt like a ghost. I do sometimes when I walk through crowded city streets. This was different; we weren't moving anywhere. The faces passing by were all blank. No one looked at us and no one was helping the people in the accident either.
I had entered Los Angeles only to be stuck heading in the wrong direction. As if some god had reached down from Mount Olympus through the smog and intervened in my decision to move there. In my mind, I heard a booming voice raining down from the sky as the car sat on the median.
"Go back child. Go back to where you came from. You will only find misery here."
But I didn't listen. No one does. Kill an actor or a writer and two more appear; nothing can deter someone from making the journey. People have embarked on this adventure ever since the first film was made in the wild west of California. They came to Los Angeles seeking a better life. They suffered or succeeded the same way they do today. The story hasn't changed much over the years. At that moment, stuck on the freeway, all I could do was pray my story would be a comedy and not a tragedy.
Los Angeles is filled with transplanted artists who stay up all night finding words to express their visions and the

businessmen who find ways to curdle their dreams by day. A land of opposites, the city separates you from the world. It insulates and isolates you, and then expects you to communicate back to the world you no longer live in.

The city creeps into the bedrooms of the unfulfilled and whispers into their ears sweet nothings. It's all just teasing foreplay in attaining the true American Dream: money and attention. Neither of which mean anything, because you can gain wealth and adoration, and then watch them leave you without a goodbye.

A person can be easily distracted in Los Angeles; you have to be focused on what you want at all times. Watching others desperately clinging to their careers is its own form of entertainment in L.A. Like zebras transfixed by a lion killing one of their own, the observers are safe for the moment but not forever.

It's not blood that flows through people's veins there; it's fear. Fear their dreams will end and upon waking find themselves returned to their former lives. Broke, broken and known only as the person they used to be, or worse yet, unknown and unrecognized all together.

Nothing lasts forever. I realized that just in time; but it took the earth crumbling apart to shake me awake. It shouldn't have been that way but it was. It got to where I couldn't tell what was real anymore and all I had was my dreams.

Los Angeles floats on those dreams. Dipping and swaying with the Santa Ana winds, it's an oasis everyone knows through legends and myths. If you take this journey, you must travel across deserts that will convince you nothing good could live there. The heat waves bend and twist the skyline as you approach it. Once you reach the oasis, your mind will reject what it sees. It is full of impossibly beautiful people, endless money, and swimming pools that reflect the sun's rays in a million opulent directions.

Beware though; nothing is what it seems. Vampires lurk around every corner and live on the blood of fresh dreamers. If bitten by one of these monsters, you will slowly mutate. Disfigured, you will become one of them. Your features will change, along with your hair, eye color, accent, breasts size, waist size and personality. When it is all said and done, no one will know you, including yourself.

Everything that lives and dies is both born and killed here under the microscope of the mythic movie studio gods. They witness everyone's dreams floating by them in their mountain realm. If pleased, they breathe life into them, thereby making them a reality on earth. My reality was consumed by being stuck on that median. I could have turned back but I didn't. That was my chance to escape but I had to know it and to live it, right or wrong. Not all was lost on my journey though. As with any story worth telling, it's not what you lose along the way that matters, it's what you find.

But I'm getting ahead of myself. I need to start at the beginning, or at least as close to the beginning that makes sense.

So as they say, once upon a time...

* * *

Also by Sebastian J. Howley

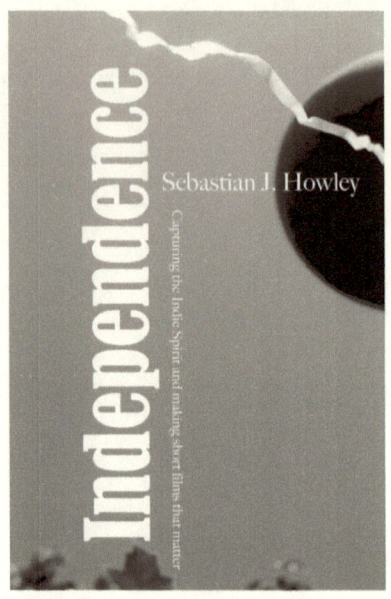

Independence:
Capturing the Indie Spirit and making short films that matter

A straightforward guide to making short films with meaning and personal importance. This book walks you through the process of finding the inspiration for creating short films that are both unique and powerful.

Sebastian J. Howley is a writer and filmmaker.

He follows a strict health regimen in hopes of living long enough to see the Chicago Cubs win the World Series.

For more information about his production company go to: www.anymomentproductions.com

He can be contacted at: info@anymomentproductions.com